Anonymous

Macaulay's Dialogues for Young People on Various Subjects and in Different Styles

Anonymous

Macaulay's Dialogues for Young People on Various Subjects and in Different Styles

ISBN/EAN: 9783337812027

Printed in Europe, USA, Canada, Australia, Japan

Cover: Foto ©Thomas Meinert / pixelio.de

More available books at **www.hansebooks.com**

MACAULAY'S
DIALOGUES

FOR YOUNG PEOPLE,

ON VARIOUS SUBJECTS AND IN DIFFERENT STYLES.

CONTAINING

A LARGE NUMBER OF THE MOST EXCELLENT PIECES,
ORIGINAL AND SELECTED.

ESPECIALLY FITTED FOR SCHOOLS, ACADEMIES, SOCIABLE GATH-
ERINGS, HOLIDAY MEETINGS, ANNIVERSARIES,
COMMENCEMENTS, PARLOR ENTER-
TAINMENTS, ETC, ETC.

NEW YORK:
ROBERT M. DE WITT, PUBLISHER,
No. 33 Rose Street.

CONTENTS

OF

MACAULAY'S DIALOGUES FOR YOUNG PEOPLE.

Name.	Author.	Page.
Agility (Dickens Charade)	G. B. Bartlett	87
America's Birthday Party	George B. Bartlett	165
Army and Navy, The	Anon	97
Apron (an Acting Charade)	L. Annie Frost	19
Bluebird and Oriole	Anon	72
Candidate for Congress, The	Anon	74
Centennial Drama, A	Mrs. E. D. Cheney	155
Chief's Resolve, The	Anon	116
City and Country	Mrs. E. B. P.	40
Columbia's Daughters	John Keynton	167
Consider the Lilies	M. B. C. Slade.	70
Discontented Girls, The	Anon	192
Excitement at Kettleville, The	Epes Sargent	63
Gridiron, The	Anon	189
Hard to Suit All	Anon	53
Imaginary Possessions	Anon	187
Little Red Riding-Hood	George Cooper	78
Love of Country	Anon	93
Lochiel's Warning	Campbell	147

Name.	Author.	Page.
Maine (Acting Charade)	M. B. C. SLADE	43
May-Basket Army, The	ANON	182
Mistletoe Bough, The	ANON	13
Money-Digger, The	H. ELLIOT M'BRIDE	30
Nature's Heroes	BEAUMONT & FLETCHER	44
Old Flag, The	ANON	107
Our Centennial	ANON	136
Our Country's Seasons	ANON	178
Peterkins, The	LUCRETIA P. HALE	8
Play of the Alphabet	ELLEN O. PECK	7
Sailor Boy's Return, The	ANON	152
Sailor's Mother, The	ANON	26
Shall our Mothers Vote?	ANON	102
Spirit of '76, The	ANON	123
Story, The	ANON	33
The Bee, the Ant, and the Spider	Mrs. LOUISA P. HOPKINS	16
True to His Colors	ANON	95
Seven	ANON	92
Uncle Nathan's Indian	ANON	179
Uncle Sam	ANON	150
Veteran, The	ANON	120
Visions of Freedom, The	ANON	129
William Tell	ANON	125
1776–1876	ANON	112

MACAULAY'S
DIALOGUES FOR YOUNG PEOPLE.

PLAY OF THE ALPHABET.

ELLEN O. PECK.

[*An exercise for twenty-six small children, the letter each represents being pinned in front of him. The last half is addressed to the audience. They take their places one by one.*]

First (*taking place on stage*). A advances.
Second (*boy coming to A's side and bowing*). B bows.
Third (*girl coming into line and dropping a courtesy*). C courtesies.
Fourth (*dancing into line*). D dances.
Fifth (*eating*). E eats.
Sixth (*coming on slowly and thoughtfully*). F forgets.
Seventh (*crying*). G grieves.
Eighth (*coming on very fast*). H hurries.
Ninth (*scrutinizing the others*). I inspects.
Tenth (*jumping along*). J jumps.
Eleventh (*coming forward and kneeling in line*). K kneels.
Twelfth (*coming quickly, lifts K up*). L lifts.
Thirteenth (*marching promptly*). M marches.
Fourteenth (*bowing*). N nods.
Fifteenth (*glancing about*). O observes.
Sixteenth (*playing on mouth-organ or jewsharp*). P plays.
Seventeenth (*holding in one hand an interrogation point*). Q questions.

Eighteenth (running into line). R runs.
Nineteenth (looking very pleasantly). S smiles.
Twentieth (coming on awkwardly, falls down). T tumbles.
Twenty-first (following quickly, helps him up). U upholds.
Twenty-second (sauntering in). V visits.
Twenty-third (bringing a book). W works.
Twenty-fourth (bringing two books). X excels.
Twenty-fifth (handing a book to X). Y yields.
Twenty-sixth (coming in an irregular course). Z zigzags.

First. Amuse us.
Second. Bless us.
Third. Care for us.
Fourth. Defend us.
Fifth. Educate us.
Sixth. Forgive us.
Seventh. Guide us.
Eighth. Help us.
Ninth. Interest us.
Tenth. Judge us.
Eleventh. Know us.
Twelfth. Love us.
Thirteenth. Mould us.
Fourteenth. Nourish us.
Fifteenth. Oblige us.
Sixteenth. Pet us.
Seventeenth. Question us.
Eighteenth. Rouse us.
Nineteenth. Steady us.
Twentieth. Trust us.
Twenty-first. Use us.
Twenty-second. Value us.
Twenty-third. Warn us.
Twenty-fourth. Excuse us.
Twenty-five. Yearn over us.
Twenty-sixth. Zest our work.

All in concert. And together we will do
Almost everything for you.

THE PETERKINS.

LUCRETIA P. HALE.

Dramatis Personæ.—AMANDA, AMANDA'S MOTHER, GIRLS OF THE GRADUATING CLASS, MRS. PETERKIN, ELIZABETH ELIZA.

Amanda (coming in with a few graduates). Mother, the exhibition is over, and I have brought the whole class home to the collation.

Mother. The whole class! But I only expected a few.

Amanda. The rest are coming. I brought Julie and Clara and Sophie with me. (*a voice is heard*) Here are the rest.

Mother. Why, no. It is Mrs. Peterkin and Elizabeth Eliza!

Amanda. Too late for the exhibition. Such a shame! But in time for the collation.

Mother (*to herself*). If the ice-cream will go round!

Amanda. But what made you so late? Did you miss the train? This is Elizabeth Eliza, girls—you have heard me speak of her. What a pity you were too late!

Mrs. Peterkin. We tried to come; we did our best.

Mother. Did you miss the train? Didn't you get my postal-card?

Mrs. Peterkin. We had nothing to do with the train.

Amanda. You don't mean you walked?

Mrs. Peterkin. Oh no, indeed!

Elizabeth Eliza. We came in a horse and carryall.

Julia. I always wondered how anybody could come in a horse!

Amanda. You are too foolish, Julie. They came in the carry-all part. But didn't you start in time?

Mrs. P. It all comes from the carryall being so hard to turn. I told Mr. Peterkin we should get into trouble with one of those carryalls that don't turn easy.

Elizabeth. They turn easy enough in the stable, so you can't tell.

Mrs. P. Yes; we started with the little boys and Solomon John on the back seat, and Elizabeth Eliza on the front. She was to drive, and I was to see to the driving. But the horse was not faced toward Boston.

Mother. And you tipped over in turning round! Oh, what an accident!

Amanda. And the little boys—where are they? Are they killed?

Elizabeth. The little boys are all safe. We left them at the Pringles', with Solomon John.

Mother. But what did happen?

Mrs. P. We started the wrong way.

Mother. You lost your way, after all?

Elizabeth. No; we knew the way well enough.

Amanda. It's as plain as a pike-staff!

Mrs. P. No; we had the horse faced in the wrong direction, toward Providence.

Elizabeth. And mother was afraid to have me turn, and we kept on and on till we should reach a wide place.

Mrs. P. I thought we should come to a road that would veer off to the right or left, and bring us back to the right direction.

Mother. Could not you all get out and turn the thing round?

Mrs. P. Why, no; if it had broken down we should not have been in anything, and could not have gone anywhere.

Elizabeth. Yes, I have always heard it was best to stay in the carriage whatever happens.

Julia. But nothing seemed to happen.

Mrs. P. Oh, yes; we met one man after another, and we asked the way to Boston.

Elizabeth. And all they would say was, "Turn right round— you are on the road to Providence."

Mrs. P. As if we could turn right round! That was just what we couldn't.

Mother. You don't mean you kept on all the way to Providence?

Elizabeth. O dear, no! We kept on and on, till we met a man with a black hand-bag—black leather I should say.

Julia. He must have been a book-agent.

Mrs. P. I dare say he was; his bag seemed heavy. He set it on a stone.

Mother. I dare say it was the same one that came here the other day. He wanted me to buy the "History of the Aborigines, brought up from earliest times to the present date," in four volumes. I told him I hadn't time to read so much. He said that was no matter, few did, and it wasn't much worth it—they bought books for the look of the thing.

Amanda. Now, that was illiterate; he never could have graduated. I hope, Elizabeth Eliza, you had nothing to do with that man.

Elizabeth. Very likely it was not the same one.

Mother. Did he have a kind of pepper-and-salt suit, with one of the buttons worn?

Mrs. P. I noticed one of the buttons was off.

Amanda. We're off the subject. Did you buy his book?

Elizabeth. He never offered us his book.

Mrs. P. He told us the same story—we were going to Providence; if we wanted to go to Boston, we must turn directly round.

Elizabeth. I told him I couldn't; but he took the horse's head, and the first thing I knew——

Amanda. He had yanked you round!

Mrs. P. I screamed; I couldn't help it!

Elizabeth. I was glad when it was over!

Mother. Well, well; it shows the disadvantage of starting wrong.

Mrs. P. Yes, we came straight enough when the horse was headed right, but we lost time.

Elizabeth. I am sorry enough I lost the exhibition, and seeing you take the diploma, Amanda. I never got the diploma myself. I came near it.

Mrs. P. Somehow, Elizabeth Eliza never succeeded. I think there was partiality about the promotions.

Elizabeth. I never was good about remembering things. I studied well enough, but, when I came to say off my lesson, I couldn't think what it was. Yet I could have answered some of the other girls' questions.

Julia. It's odd how the other girls always have the easiest questions.

Elizabeth. I never could remember poetry. There was only one thing I could repeat.

Amanda. Oh, do let us have it now; and then we'll recite to you some of our exhibition pieces.

Elizabeth. I'll try.

Mrs. P. Yes, Elizabeth Eliza, do what you can to help entertain Amanda's friends. (*all stand looking at* ELIZABETH ELIZA, *who remains silent and thoughtful.*)

Elizabeth. I'm trying to think what it is about. You all know it. You remember, Amanda—the name is rather long.

Amanda. It can't be Nebuchadnezzar, can it?—that is one of the longest names I know.

Elizabeth. Oh dear, no!

Julia. Perhaps it's Cleopatra.

Elizabeth. It does begin with a " C "—only he was a boy.

Amanda. That's a pity, for it might be " We are seven," only that is a girl. Some of them were boys.

Elizabeth. It begins about a boy—if I could only think where he was. I can't remember.

Amanda. Perhaps he " stood upon the burning deck ? "

Elizabeth. That's just it; I knew he stood somewhere.

Amanda. Casabianca ! Now begin—go ahead !

Elizabeth.
>" The boy stood on the burning deck,
>When—when——"

I can't think who stood there with him.

Julia. If the deck was burning, it must have been on fire. I guess the rest ran away, or jumped into boats.

Amanda. That's just it.
>" Whence all but him had fled."

Elizabeth. I think I can say it now.
>" The boy stood on the burning deck,
>Whence all but him had fled—"

(*she hesitates*) Then I think he went——

Julia. of course, he fled after the rest.

Amanda. Dear, no ! That's the point. He didn't.
>" The flames rolled on, he would not go
>Without his father's word."

Elizabeth. Oh, yes. Now I can say it.
>" The boy stood on the burning deck,
>Whence all but him had fled ;
>The flames rolled on, he would not go
>Without his father's word."

But it used to rhyme. I don't know what has happened to it.

Mrs. P. Elizabeth Eliza is very particular about the rhymes.

Elizabeth. It must be " without his father's *head*," or, perhaps, " without his father *said* " he should.

Julia. I think you must have omitted something.

Amanda. She has left out ever so much!

Mother. Perhaps it's as well to omit some, for the ice-cream has come, and you must all come down.

Amanda. And here are the rest of the girls; and let us all unite in a song! (*Exeunt, singing.*)

THE MISTLETOE BOUGH.

[Arranged for Parlor or School Representation as a Ballad with Living Pictures.]

The well-known story of "Ginevra," as told in Rogers' poem of "Italy," and in the ballad of "The Mistletoe Bough," is very suitable for parlor representation, especially during the Christmas holidays. To give it with the best effect, a temporary stage and drop-curtain are needed; better still if the curtain be hung at the wide opening between two rooms. As an expedient, two large clothes-horses, draped and stood so as to form the back and sides of the stage—thus, ⸺ ⸺, answer the purpose admirably. The flooring of the stage should, if practicable, be raised about fourteen inches. A large pine frame covered with gilt or "black walnut" paper, if placed close to the stage so as to form a picture-frame to each scene, will add very much to the illusion; and the effect will be still finer if a very thin black gauze or tarletan be stretched across the back of the frame over the entire opening. But both the frame and gauze may be dispensed with if they involve too much painstaking. In any case, a sliding curtain can be hung on a wire stretched across the front, and so arranged as to be drawn back, when necessary, by persons concealed at each end of the screen. A space can be left in the rear, between the two clothes-horses, where the actors, by parting the draperies, may go in and out. Somebody behind the screen recites or sings the ballad, which at proper intervals is illustrated by *tableaux vivants*. Everything must be arranged in advance, and the actors dressed ready to appear. A large wooden chest should be at hand. It may stand in the rear of the stage in the first scene, concealed by gay draperies or the wedding guests. A capital chest may be made of large sheets of pasteboard sewed together and covered with oak wall-paper. Great iron hinges and locks should be painted upon it. The lid, bent down around the edge, can be tied on at the back, so as to open and shut. The mistletoe bough and holly, if necessary, can be made of green paper; or almost any green boughs with small leaves will answer the purpose. The costumes, which in detail may be left to the taste of the performers, should have an old-time effect and be in harmony with each other. The chief requirements are powdered heads, knee-breeches, and great shoe-buckles for the gentlemen; high-heeled and rosetted slippers, farthingales, trains, puffed, curled and powdered heads, with flowers, wreaths, and showy jewelry for the ladies. Twenty-five cents' worth of tinsel paper, crinkled and creased, will greatly assist in the jewelry and shoe-buckle effects, when better things are not at hand. Old chintz curtains for the guests, and muslin or lace curtains for the bride, will make capital trains and mantles; white wool-wadding and horse-hair will serve for the ladies' and gentlemen's wigs, when powder is not used, and knee-breeches may be easily produced by cutting the bottoms off of old trousers, lapping them tightly at the knee, and concealing the lap by a rosette. Two persons may be required to represent Lovel—one as a young, the other as an old man. For the latter part, a long white beard may be made of goat's-hair fringe or white wool-wadding. A few charcoal shadows about the face (studied from nature) will produce the look of old age. In the last scene, the wedding guests, with a few slight changes of costume, and with charcoal shadows on some of the faces, will serve as the old man's friends. Children can personate all the characters as easily as grown persons.

A spinning wheel and a few old-style pieces of furniture will be found useful.

Very pleasing results, however, can be secured with far less preparation than we have suggested. The main thing is to try for harmonious effects of color and grouping, and the proper lighting up of the tableaux. All the lights should be in front of the performers, and hidden from the spectators. If the scenes are carefully rehearsed there will be no difficulty in arranging each tableau silently and swiftly in its proper succession. Actual experiment will be the best guide in deciding at which points the curtain is to be raised and lowered. When practicable, the singing or reciting of each stanza should accompany its tableau to the fall of the curtain, and the music accompaniment can run on between the stanzas during the brief time allowed for arranging each scene.

TABLEAU I.

The mistletoe hung in the castle hall,
The holly branch shone on the old oak wall;
And the baron's retainers were blithe and gay,
And keeping their Christmas holiday.
The baron beheld with a father's pride
His beautiful daughter, young Lovel's bride,
While she with her bright eyes seemed to be
The star of that goodly company.
  Oh! the mistletoe bough!
  Oh! the mistletoe bough!

TABLEAU. SCENE.—*The castle hall. The happy old baron and baroness are seated in state; the bride and groom, with the wed-*

ding guests, may be represented as dancing, or in the act of playing some merry game.

TABLEAU II.

"I'm weary of dancing now," she cried;
"Here tarry a moment—I'll hide, I'll hide!
And Lovel be sure thou'rt the first to trace
The clue to my secret lurking-place."
Away she ran, and her friends began
Each tower to search, and each nook to scan;
And young Lovel cried, "Oh, where dost thou hide?
I'm lonesome without thee, my own dear bride."
Oh! the mistletoe, etc.

TABLEAU. *Curtain rises at "Away she ran."* SCENE.—*A dim old garret. When there are no painted scenes, this effect is produced by lowering the lights and displaying dimly a few old chairs, garments, and stray articles, crowded together at one side; while at the other, nearer to the centre, stands the large open chest. The floor should be of dark boards or covered with some dull material. Ginevra, drawing her wedding drapery around her, and looking merrily back, is about stepping into the chest. The light should be arranged so as to fall only upon the form of Ginevra.*

TABLEAU III.

They sought her that night, and they sought her next day,
And they sought her in vain when a week pass'd away;
In the highest, the lowest, the loneliest spot,
Young Lovel sought wildly, but found her not.
And years flew by, and their grief at last
Was told as a sorrowful tale long past;
And when Lovel appeared, the children cried:
"See! the old man weeps for his fairy bride!"
Oh! the mistletoe, etc.

PANTOMIME. *Curtain rises at "And years flew by." An out-of-door scene. (If the trunk and various articles are pushed back and covered with green baize, and groups of children, with hats on, are arranged to partially conceal the background, a painted scene can be dispensed with.) Lovel, now an old man with long white beard, with cocked hat, and big cane, is seen walking slowly across the stage from* L. *His head is bowed and his manner very sad. The children, looking pityingly at him, whisper together, and, finally, two or three steal up to him, as if to attract his attention, as the curtain falls.*

TABLEAU IV.

> At length an oak chest, that had long lain hid,
> Was found in the castle—they raised the lid,
> And a skeleton form lay mouldering there,
> In the bridal wreath of the lady fair!
> Oh! sad was her fate! in sportive jest
> She hid from her lord in the old oak chest.
> It closed with a spring, and her bridal bloom
> Lay withering there in a living tomb!
>   Oh! the mistletoe, etc.

TABLEAU. *Curtain rises at* "*Sad was her fate.*" SCENE.—*The garret as before. Lovel, the old man, stands near the open chest, grief-stricken, with a necklace in his hand. A group of friends stand by in amazement and pity. One young girl has her arm on Lovel's shoulder, as if to gently draw him away.* (*Curtain fall while the music is playing.*)

THE BEE, THE ANT, AND THE SPIDER.

MRS. LOUISA P. HOPKINS.

Spider. How pleasant, while upborne on airy wave,
            To spread my laces, spin my threads, and save
            The pearly dews that glisten in the morn,
            My fairy robes of gossamer to adorn.
            How nice to weave my cunning, spiral trap,
            And then, with one eye open, take my nap.

Bee.   Buzz! buzz! I am well called the busy Bee;
            The sun comes up, the flowers bloom for me.
            I'll fly about, and load my hairy legs
            With pollen-dust, to feed my larvæ eggs,

	Then pack it in my saddle-bags, and tax
	The generous flowers again, for plates of wax,
	And suck up honey from their nectared wells,
	To hoard within my curious, six-walled cells.
Ant.	There goes the noisy Bee; what endless hum
	Announces all his pompous folks! they come
	With fuss and wings, while I, more modest, creep
	Quiet and business-like, about my heap;
	Mine out my galleries, and raise my dome,
	Patient and tireless, while I rear my home.
	Well, flying is my pastime once a year;
	I'll take my wedding-flight when July's here.
	All over, then the useless wings I doff,
	And go to work when I have pulled them off.
Spider.	Now, starting from my hiding-place, so nimble,
	I'll take my thread and needle (where's my thimble?),
	A fly is struggling through my breaking net;
	As I'm alert, I hope to have him yet.
	I'll tie him down, laugh at his frantic buzz,
	And suck his blood, as every victor does!
	Then, at my leisure, knit my silken bag
	To hang my eggs in, while the seasons wag.
Bee.	I'll rifle all the roses, this bright day,
	My brother takes the tulips on his way;
	For each wise bee seeks only kindred flowers,
	Conserving one pure nectar through the hours;
	From like corolla to corolla flies,
	Till, with his honeyed burden, home he hies.
Ant.	Such hosts of sweet Aphides we have found,
	We'll drive them to our safe folds, underground;
	We see them crowded, green beneath the leaves,
	To gather juices for us lucky thieves!
	Or on the oak-trees, sucking sap so good,
	We follow them, and tap them for our food.
Bee.	What social, happy, thriving tribes are we,
	With fanning wings and talking antennæ!

We meet in merry flight, and homeward go;
How far so'er our hives, the way we know,
Take the bee-line, nor drop our precious load,
But haste, like courtiers, on our sunny road.

Ant. In Africa our legionaries rear
Their towering palaces, and brave men fear
Their hosted swarms, marching o'er wasted leagues;
With military skill, and fierce intrigues,
They storm, besiege, attack, and capture foes,
With slaves reward their generalissimos,
Honor their Cæsars and Napoleons,
Attend their living, or caress their bones.
They knew the tactics ere the schools had taught,
And do by instinct what world-heroes wrought.

Spider. I can show men true patience and cantrivance,
What may be done by art and wise connivance.
Better than looms my wondrous spinning-pockets,
Swifter than weaver's shuttle, or than rockets,
I twist my shining threads, and shoot my lines,
Till nadir with circumference, all entwines,
And fine and firm my castle walls are made,
With outworks and defences truly laid.

Bee. How learned we then the secret of our art,
To build our perfect cells, to play our part,
Our eggs to nourish rightly, and prepare
Just what each needs, with such sagacious care?
What voice directs our Queen to ardent fight,
And calls to tournament each eager knight?
What clarion notes draw forth the lively swarm,
In loyal zeal new colonies to form?

Ant. How swiftly fly the hazy summer days!
Each rosy hour rolls on its busy ways,
While some kind power our lesson to us reads,
And gives each one the wisdom that he needs,
Informs the Bee, and Ant, and Spider, too,
Its own best life to live and truest work to do.

APRON (an Acting Charade).

L. ANNIE FROST.

Characters.—CLARENCE BALDWIN, CHARLOTTE BALDWIN, VICTOR SOMERSET, WALTER BALDWIN, *and* VICTOR'S APE.*

SCENE I. (*Ape.*)

SCENE.—*A sitting-room. In one corner a stand of flowers. Upon a table, writing materials and a work-basket, with sewing materials. Over a chair is thrown a long cloak, and a bonnet upon it. An etagére, with the usual ornaments. A large mirror in background, and a sham window, thrown open. Everything is arranged in a very orderly manner.*

Curtain rises, discovering CLARENCE *seated, ciphering upon a slate ;* CHARLOTTE *drawing a map upon paper.*

Charlotte. There! I have finished my map. I think Maine is the most tiresome of all the States to draw, the coast is so irregular.

Clarence. I wish my sum was finished. I can't make it come right.

Enter WALTER.

Walter. Oh, Claire! Lottie! Victor Somerset is coming in a few minutes to bring Jocko.

Clarence. Jocko?

Walter. Oh! I forgot, Claire, that you had been away since Jocko came.

Clarence. But who is Jocko? I never heard of anything but a monkey being named Jocko.

Walter. You've guessed it the first time. Jocko is a Barbary

---

* The costume for an ape can easily be obtained in a city at a costumer's; but in the country some ingenuity will be required to make a flexible mask and a plain-fitting suit of brown shaggy cloth for the character.

ape, as tall as his master. Victor's uncle sent him to him, and he has been taught all sorts of funny tricks.

Charlotte. I shall be afraid of him.

Walter. Pshaw! he wont hurt you. He is perfectly tame.

Enter VICTOR *and ape; the ape has a string around his waist, by which* VICTOR *leads him.*

Victor. Good morning!

Walter. Good morning! We are very glad to see you. So this is Jocko?

Victor. Yes. Shake hands, Jocko. (JOCKO *shakes hands, in monkey style, with* WALTER *and* CLARENCE.)

Charlotte. I'm afraid! (*runs out of reach of* JOCKO, *leaving her map on her chair.* JOCKO *tugs at the string to follow her.*)

Victor. For shame, sir! Kiss your hand to the lady. (JOCKO *kisses his hand to* CHARLOTTE.)

Charlotte. Oh, what a funny fellow!

Walter. Isn't he splendid? Make him do something else, wont you, Victor?

Clarence (*putting his slate and pencil on table*). O yes! please make him, Victor.

Victor. Make a bow, sir. (JOCKO *bows very low.*)

Walter. Would he mind me? Shake hands, Jocko. (JOCKO *puts both paws behind his back.*)

Clarence (*laughing*). He knows his master, Walter.

Victor. Sit down in that chair (JOCKO *sits down.*)

Clarence. What a grand pet!

Victor. Go to sleep. (JOCKO *lies down on the floor and shuts his eyes.* VICTOR *sits down near him.*)

Clarence. Have you had him long, Victor?

Victor. Nearly a month. Uncle John had him trained expressly for me. I don't think he has one vicious trick. (JOCKO *slyly picks an apple from* VICTOR'S *pocket, bites a piece out, and puts it back, unperceived*)

Walter. Do you have to keep him tied up?

Victor. I do now, but I hope to train him to respect property, so that he can run at large (JOCKO *steals another bite of apple.*)

Charlotte. Does he never bite you?

Victor. Never. He tears and destroys furniture and clothing, but he is never savage. (JOCKO *again steals the apple, and eats it all.*)

Victor. Sit up, sir. Hulloo! Where did you get that apple? (JOCKO *grins, and hastily munches and swallows the last bite.*)

Charlotte. He stole it out of your pocket.

Victor. I owe you a whipping, sir. (JOCKO *makes gestures of fear.*)

Walter. Oh, don't whip him! I'll give him an apple.

Victor. I wont whip you this time then. (JOCKO *makes gestures of delight.*)

Clarence. What else can he do, Victor?

Victor. Oh, he can walk on all fours! Walk like a dog, sir! (JOCKO *walks on all fours, and runs at* CHARLOTTE, *who retreats into a corner,* JOCKO *chattering at her.*)

Victor. Here, come back, sir. (JOCKO *tugs at string.*)

Victor. Shake hands with him, Lottie. He wont hurt you.

Charlotte. Are you sure he wont bite?

Victor. Certain of it. (CHARLOTTE *comes forward, timidly*) Stand up, and shake hands with the lady, sir. (JOCKO *stands up, takes* CHARLOTTE'S *hand, and kisses it, chattering his teeth at her.*)

Victor. Sit down life a tailor. (JOCKO *sits on the floor, cross-legged*) Smoke a pipe. (*hands a pipe to* JOCKO, *who pretends to smoke it. Bell rings.*)

Walter. Oh, there's the dinner bell! Do stay to dinner, Victor!

Clarence. Yes, stay, Victor! Can't you tie Jocko?

Victor. Certainly I can. (*ties* JOCKO *to the handle of the door*) There, he cannot do any mischief now. I will show you the rest of his tricks after dinner. (*curtain falls.*)

SCENE II. (*Run.*)

SCENE.—*Same as before. Curtain rises, discovering* JOCKO *alone, pulling the string on the door. The string snaps, leaving him free* JOCKO *walks all round the room, grinning and chattering his teeth. He takes* CLARENCE'S *slate, and rubs the sum all out with with his paw. He puts* CHARLOTTE'S *map over his head, tearing a hole and wearing it like a ruff.*

He turns all the flower-pots upside down. He spies himself in the mirror, and dances before it, bowing and grinning. He upsets all the chairs, and finally, after removing the articles from the etagére, and putting them on the middle of the floor with many a monkeyish motion, turns it over with a grand crash.

CLARENCE, VICTOR, *and* WALTER *run in.*

Clarence. Oh, Victor! he has broken loose.

Victor (*sternly*). Come here, sir. (JOCKO *grins and chatters.*)

Walter (*laughing*). You said you would show us some more of his tricks after dinner! Just look at the room!

Clarence. I think he has been his own showman.

Victor (*stamping his foot*). Come here, sir. (JOCKO *jumps on the sofa.*)

Walter. How can you catch him?

Victor. Oh, I can catch him! Come here, sir, or I will whip you. (JOCKO *jumps down behind the sofa, and grins over the back at* VICTOR. VICTOR *runs toward him*) I'll teach you to act so. (JOCKO *runs round the room,* VICTOR *after him, overturning furniture and making all the confusion possible.*)

Walter. Go it! Catch him, Victor Run, Jocko!

Clarence. Can't he run? (JOCKO *jumps through the window;* VICTOR *follows him.*)

Walter (*running to window*). Oh, see them, Claire! There goes Jocko right into the fountain! Now he is out! (*shouting*) Run, Victor, run!

Clarence (*looking from window*). Oh, Walter, he has broken mamma's china jars with the lemon trees! Did you ever see anything run so fast? He has been all round the garden four or five times already.

Walter. There he goes up a tree! Victor is all out of breath, but he is coaxing him down.

Clarence. Jocko wont be coaxed.

Walter. There goes Victor up the tree.

Clarence. But not so quickly as Jocko jumps down. Now for another run!

Walter (*laughing*). Ha! ha! ha! I never saw such a race. (*claps his hands*) Victor is no match for Jocko!

Clarence. There! He has jumped over the fence. See him run down the road! He will be out of sight before Victor gets the gate open!

Walter. No, it is open now. He is turning the wrong way. (*calling from window*) Run to the right! run to the right!

Clarence. He hears you. Run, Victor, run!

Both (*clapping their hands and shouting*). Run! run! run! (*curtain falls.*)

SCENE III. (*Apron.*)

SCENE.—*Same as Scene I. Curtain rises, discovering* CHARLOTTE *folding an apron.*

Charlotte. I believe the room is all in order now. What a mess Jocko did make! I will fold this apron and put it on mamma's work-basket. How fortunate it was he did not touch that! (*folds apron and puts it on basket*) I wonder if mamma has done with her cloak and bonnet? I will go ask her, before I put them away.

(*Exit* CHARLOTTE.)

Walter (*behind the scene*). Oh, Victor, I hope you have not lost him! Come to my room, and rest.

A moment's pause, then JOCKO *climbs upon the window-seat and looks in. He peeps all round the room, and finally comes in, very slowly and cautiously. He goes all over the room, looking under the chairs and table, and finally sits down facing audience, and fans himself with* CLARENCE'S *slate. After sitting gravely a moment he pulls the work-basket toward him, and begins to pull the things out; unwinds the spools of cotton, throws the emery-bag and pin-cushion on the floor, and takes out the scissors. First he pricks his fingers with them, then smells them and pricks his nose; then takes a book off the table, punches holes in the cover, and snips the leaves. He unrolls the apron and surveys it; finally bundles it up and throws it at the chair where the cloak and bonnet are lying. He springs up suddenly and runs to the chair, puts on the cloak and bonnet, and goes to the mirror; here he bows, smirks, and strikes attitudes. He takes up the apron again, and the scissors.*

Clarence (behind the scenes). Come in here, Victor, and we will hold a consultation.

JOCKO *runs into a corner and sits down in a chair, face to wall, drawing the cloak close around him. During the conversation following he turns his face occasionally toward audience and grins, unperceived by the speakers, who must sit facing audience.*

Enter VICTOR, CLARENCE, *and* WALTER.

Victor. I am afraid he jumped upon some cart that was passing, and so I have lost him entirely.
Walter. Oh, I hope not.
Clarence. You will have to advertise him.
Walter. You may get him then if you offer a handsome reward.
Victor. And pay expenses. Who knows how much mischief he has done! Just think of the confusion he made here!
Clarence. Oh, that's no matter! Lottie said there was not much real harm done. My sum and her map will have to be copied again; but I am sure the amusement he gave us paid for that trouble.
Victor. Sitting here will not find him; but I am almost tired out. I shall be stiff for a week after that race.
Walter. You must rest a little while.
Victor. If I ever do catch Jocko he shall have a chain, and a good strong one too. (JOCKO *shakes his fist at* VICTOR.)
Clarence. Oh, I do hope you will catch him! Perhaps he will come home himself. Dogs do sometimes when they are lost.

Enter CHARLOTTE.

Charlotte. Why! who upset mamma's work-basket? (*picks up the things and puts them in basket.*)
Walter (rising). I must go. I have an errand to do for father before dark.

Victor. I must go too, and consult father about Jocko.

(*Exeunt* WALTER, CLARENCE, *and* VICTOR.)

Charlotte (*seeing* JOCKO). What is mamma sitting over there for? Is she going out again? Mamma! mamma! (JOCKO *begins to cut the apron with scissors*) Oh, mamma! what are you cutting my new apron all to pieces for? (JOCKO *turns and grins at her.* CHARLOTTE *screams*) Oh, it's that horrid ape! Victor! Walter! (*runs toward door.* JOCKO *jumps up and catches her.* CHARLOTTE *screams, and* JOCKO *ties up her mouth with the apron.* CHARLOTTE *struggles*) Oh, let me go! let me go!

Enter WALTER, CLARENCE, *and* VICTOR. VICTOR *runs quickly behind* JOCKO, *and catches his arms.*

Charlotte (*untying the apron*). Have you got him fast?

Clarence. Here, tie him with this piece of string he left on the door until you get a chain.

Victor (*tying* JOCKO). You won't escape me again in a hurry. What have you got to say for yourself, sir? (JOCKY *hangs his head*) Are you sorry, sir? (*takes off the cloak and bonnet.* JOCKO *nods two or three times.*)

Walter. I really believe he understands every word you say. (JOCKO *nods and grins.*)

Victor. Now come home, sir, and stay in your cage until I buy you a chain. Make a bow to the lady and gentlemen, Jocko. (JOCKO *bows.*)

Victor. Good-bye, all!

All. Good-bye!

Walter. I will go with you. It is in my way.

(*Exeunt* VICTOR, WALTER, *and* JOCKO.)

Clarence. Why, Lottie! what makes you look so doleful? Did he hurt you?

Charlotte. No. But just look at this! *holds up apron to show the holes cut by* JOCKO.)

Clarence. Whew! rather spoiled, Lottie! But never mind; we've had fun enough with Jocko to more than make up for it. (*Curtain falls.*)

THE SAILOR'S MOTHER.

[*The woman to be represented dressed as an elderly person. She displays emotion.*]

Woman.

Sir, for the love of God, some small relief
To a poor woman!

Traveller.

Whither are you bound?
'Tis a late hour to travel o'er these downs—
No house for miles around us, and the way
Dreary and wild. The evening wind already
Makes one's teeth chatter; and the very sun,
Setting so pale behind those thin white clouds,
Looks cold. 'Twill be a bitter night!

Woman.

Aye, sir,
'Tis cutting keen! I smart at ev'ry breath :—
Heaven knows how I shall reach my journey's end;
For the way is long before me, and my feet—
God help me!—sore with travelling. I would gladly,
If it pleased God, at once lie down and die.

Traveller.

Nay, nay, cheer up! a little food and rest
Will comfort you; and then your journey's end
May make amends for all. You shake your head,
And weep. Is it some mournful business, then,
That leads you from your home?

Woman.

Sir, I am going
To see my son at Plymouth, sadly hurt
In the late action, and in the hospital
Dying, I fear me, now.

Traveller.

          He yet may live.
But if the worst should chance, why, you must bear
The will of Heaven with patience. Were it not
Some comfort to reflect your son has fallen
Fighting his country's cause? and for yourself,
You will not in unpitied poverty
Be left to mourn his loss. Your grateful country,
Amid the triumph of her victory,
Remembers those who paid its price of blood,
And with a noble charity relieves
The widow and the orphan.

Woman.

                God reward them!
God bless them! It will help me in my age.
But, sir, it will not pay me for my child!

Traveller.

Was he your only child?

Woman.

           My only one—
The stay and comfort of my widowhood!—
A dear good boy! When first he went to sea,
I felt what it would come to:—something told me
I should be childless soon. But tell me, sir,
If it be true that for a hurt like his
There is no cure. Please God to spare his life,
Though he be blind, yet I should be so thankful!
I can remember there was a blind man
Lived in our village—one, from his youth up,
Quite dark;—and yet he was a merry man;
And he had none to tend on him so well
As I would tend my boy!

Traveller.

             Of this be sure:
His hurts are looked to well; and the best help
The land affords—as rightly is due—

Ever at hand. How happened it he left you?
Was a seafaring life his early choice?

Woman.

No, sir : poor fellow !—he was wise enough
To be content at home ; and 'twas a home
As comfortable, sir, even though I say it,
As any in the country. He was left
A little boy, when his poor father died—
Just old enough to totter by himself,
And call his mother's name. We two were all ;
And as we were not left quite destitute,
We bore up well. In the summer-time I worked
Sometimes afield. Then I was famed for knitting,
And in long winter nights my spinning-wheel
Seldom stood still. We had kind neighbors too,
And never felt distress. So he grew up
A comely lad, and wondrous well disposed.
I taught him well : there was not in the parish
A child who said his prayers more regular,
Or answered readier through his catechism.
If I had foreseen this !—but 'tis a blessing
We don't know what we're born to !

Traveller.

But how came it
He chose to be a sailor ?

Woman.

You shall hear, sir.
As he grew up, he used to watch the birds
In the corn—child's work, you know, and easily done—
'Tis an idle sort of task ; so he built up
A little hut of wicker-work and clay
Under the hedge, to shelter him in rain ;
And then he took, for very idleness,
To making traps to catch the plunderers—
All sorts of cunning traps that boys can make—
Propping a stone, to fall and shut them in,
Or crush them with its weight—or else a spring

Swung on a bough. He made them cleverly;
And I—poor foolish woman!—I was pleased
To see the boy so handy. You may guess
What followed, sir, from this unlucky skill.
He did what he should not when he was older.
I warned him oft enough; but he was caught
In wiring hares at last, and had his choice—
The prison or the ship.

Traveller.

     The choice at least
Was kindly left him; and for broken laws
This was, methinks, no heavy punishment.

Woman.

So I was told, sir, and I tried to think so;
But 'twas a sad blow to me. I was used
To sleep at nights as sweetly as a child;—
Now, if the wind blew rough, it made me start,
And think of my poor boy, tossing about
Upon the roaring seas. And then I seemed
To feel that it was hard to take him from me
For such a little fault. But he was wrong,
O, very wrong—a murrain on his traps!
See what they've brought him to!

Traveller.

      Well! well! take comfort;
He will be taken care of, if he lives;
And should you lose your child, this is a country
Where the brave sailor never leaves a parent
To weep for him in want.

Woman.

    Sir, I shall want
No succor long. In the common course of years
I soon must be at rest; and 'tis a comfort,
When grief is hard upon me, to reflect
It only leads me to that rest the sooner.

THE MONEY-DIGGER.

H. ELLIOT M'BRIDE.

Characters.—Jonathan Holliday, Susannah Holliday.

PART I.

Scene.—*A room in* Jonathan Holliday's *house.* Jonathan *reading a dream-book.*

Susannah. I declare, Jonathan, you are making a right-down fool of yourself. If you would stick to your work, you would make a sight more money than you'll ever make by running after *constrologists*, and dreaming about chests of gold, and caves in the ground, and all such shaller things.

Jonathan. Now you're going on again. I tell you, Susannah, I am almost sure to find it. All the astrologists, and the fortune-tellers, and the dream-books agree that if a person dreams of money the first night of two successive months, and if he dreams of it again some time in the third month, he is sure to find it if he will only dig for it, and a pretty good pile too. Now, on the first night of last month I dreamed about a huge iron chest containing five hundred thousand dollars in gold; and on the flirst night of this month I dreamed about the same iron chest, but I didn't see the money.

Susannah. No; nor never will.

Jonathan. Yes, I will; I'm sure I will. If I dream about it any time next month I'm a rich man. And I know I *will* dream about it, for my mind will be running on it, and I can't help but dream about it. O, Susannah, then we'll go to the city and build a marble palace, and we'll ride in our carriage, and never do a bit of work.

Susannah. I declare, Jonathan, you're the greatest goose I ever did see. Who do you suppose would be fool enough to hide a chest of five hundred thousand dollars in these hills?

Jonathan. Why, the people who lived here before us might

have done it; or there might have been a great miser in this country, at one time; and he might not have wanted any person to get his money, and so he might have hid it, and never said anything about it.

Susannah. Such a thing isn't probable at all, Jonathan; and I would advise you to give it up and go to work; for I tell you plainly, if you don't, we'll soon be in a starving condition. Here I have to work my hands off every day to keep you alive, while you are doing nothing but running round hunting up fortune-tellers and reading dream-books.

Jonathan. Now, Susannah, don't go on so.

Susannah. Yes, but I will go on so; and I tell you you'll have to get down to your work again, or I'll raise a rumpus.

Jonathan. Do be quiet a little while, Susannah.

Susannah. I won't be quiet; I'm going to give you a piece of my mind. I've been wanting to do it for three or four days; and now I've got a good chance at you, and I'm going to tell you just what you are, and what you've got to do. There's got to be no more sightin' round over the country in search of caves and chests of gold, and running after fortune-tellers, and buying up dream-books. Aren't you ashamed of yourself? Now take your hammer and awl again, and peg away, and you'll make more money than you'll ever dig out of the ground, if you should dig until you are as old as Methuselah.

Jonathan. But I know I'll get the money; I feel sure of it. Where's the spade? I'm off. (*Exeunt.*)

PART II.

Scene.—*Same as first.* Jonathan *in a chair, half asleep, nodding.* Susannah *clearing away dinner-table.*

Susannah. Wake up, now, Jonathan; you've had your dinner, and you had better get those boots finished.

Jonathan. Yes. (*nods*) All gone. (*nods*) All gone.

Susannah. What's all gone? Wake up, I say.

Jonathan (*waking*). O, Susy, don't pester a body so. You know I was digging last night.

Susannah. Yes, I know; digging after a wild-goose chase. Wake up, and get to work.

Jonathan. O, Susy, can't you let a fellow have a nap, and not be whoopin' round the house in that kind of style?

Susannah. O, yes, if I'd let you alone, you'd sleep till supper-time; and goodness knows you'd better earn your supper before you eat it. Since you've been diggin' in the hills, we've got scarce of victuals and everything else.

Jonathan (yawning). Well, Susy, let me have a nap now, and I promise you there'll be no more digging for money.

Susannah. What! Will you really give it up?

Jonathan. Yes, Susy; I've come to my senses at last. I'll dig no more.

Susannah (with a sigh of relief). Well, well; I thought you intended to dig all the year; but I'm glad you've given it up.

Jonathan. I was a fool, Susy.

Susannah. That's true. You've blistered your hands, and tired your bones, and lost your sleep; but you have learned a lesson. Do you remember the proverb, Jonathan?

Jonathan (yawning). Yes, a dozen on 'em.

Susannah. Yes; but the one particularly applicable in your care?

Jonathan. O, I suppose it is, "All is not gold that glitters."

Susannah. No; think again.

Jonathan (yawning). O, you bother me so! Well, I reckon it is, "Dig not for money in the mountains."

Susannah. Why, Jonathan! that isn't a proverb. You are so dull! Here it is, and it is good advice to you (*turning to audience*) as well as to our friends here before us—"Never make haste to be rich." (*Exeunt.*)

THE STORY.

[JOSEPH, SAMUEL, REBEKAH, *and three or four others.*]

Joseph.

Have we not had "Button-Button" enough,
And "Forfeits," and all such silly stuff?

Samuel.

Well, we were playing "Blindman's-Buff"
Until you fell, and rose in a huff,
And declared the game was too rude and rough.
Poor boy! What a pity he isn't tough!

All.

Ha! ha! ha! what a pretty boy!
Papa's delight, and mamma's joy!
Wouldn't he like to go to bed,
And have a cabbage leaf on his head?

Joseph.

Laugh, if you like to! Laugh till you're gray;
But I guess you'd laugh another way
If you'd hit your toe, and fallen like me,
And cut a bloodly gash in your knee,
And bumped your nose, and bruised your shin,
Tumbling over the rolling-pin
That rolled to the floor in the awful din
That followed the fall of the row of tin
That stood upon the dresser.

Samuel.

Guess again—dear little guesser!
You wouldn't catch this boy lopping his wing,
Or whining over anything.
So stir your stumps,
Forget your bumps,
Get out of your dumps,

And up and at it again ;
For the clock is striking ten,
And Ruth will come pretty soon and say,
"Go to your beds,
You sleepy heads!"
So—quick! What shall we play?

Rebekah.

I wouldn't play any more,
For Joseph is tired and sore
With his fall upon the floor.

All.

Then he shall tell a story.

Joseph.

About old Mother Morey?

All.

No! Tell us another.

Joseph.

About my brother?

Rebekah.

Now, Joseph, you shall be good,
  And do as you'd be done by ;
We didn't mean to be rude
  When you fell and began to cry ;
We wanted to make you forget your pain ;
But it frets you, and we'll not laugh again.

Joseph.

Well, if you'll all sit still,
And not be frisking about,
Nor utter a whisper till
You've heard my story out,
I'll tell you a tale as weird
As ever you heard in your lives,
Of a man with a long blue beard,
And the way he treated his wives.

All.

Oh, that will be nice!
We'll be still as mice.

Joseph (relates the old story of Bluebeard).

Centuries since there flourished a man
(A cruel old Tartar, as rich as the Khan),
Whose castle was built on a splendid plan,
 With gardens and groves and plantations;
But his shaggy beard was as blue as the sky,
And he lived alone, for his neighbors were shy,
And had heard hard stories, by-the-by,
 About his domestic relations.

Just on the opposite side of the plain
A widow abode with her daughters twain;
And one of them—neither cross nor vain—
 Was a beautiful little treasure!
So he sent them an invitation to tea,
And having a natural wish to see
His wonderful castle and gardens, all three
 Said they'd do themselves the pleasure.

As soon as there happened a pleasant day,
They dressed themselves in a sumptuous way,
And rode to the castle as proud and gay
 As silks and jewels could make them;
And they were received in the finest style,
And saw everything that was worth their while,
In the halls of Bluebeard's grand old pile,
 Where he was so kind as to take them.

The ladies were all enchanted quite;
For they found old Bluebeard so polite
That they did not suffer at all from fright,
 And frequently called thereafter;
Then he offered to marry the younger one,
And as she was willing the thing was done,
And celebrated by all the ton
 With feasting and with laughter.

As kind a husband as ever was seen
Was Bluebeard then, for a month, I ween!
And she was as proud as any queen,
    And as happy as she could be, too;
But her husband called her to him one day,
And said, "My dear, I am going away;
It will not be long that I shall stay;
    There is business for me to see to.

"The keys of my castle I leave with you;
But if you value my love, be true,
And forbear to enter the Chamber of Blue!
    Farewell, Fatima! Remember!"
Fatima promised him; then she ran
To visit the rooms with her sister Ann;
But when she had finished the tour, she began
    To think about the Blue Chamber.

Well, the woman was curiously inclined,
So she left her sister and prudence behind
(With a little excuse) and started to find
    The mystery forbidden.
She paused at the door;—all was still as night!
She opened it: then through the dim, blue light
There blistered her vision the horrible sight
    That was in that chamber hidden.

The room was gloomy and damp and wide,
And the floor was red with the bloody tide
From headless women, laid side by side,
    The wives of her lord and master!
Frightened and fainting, she dropped the key,
But seized it and lifted it quickly; then she
Hurried as swiftly as she could flee
    From the scene of the disaster.

She tried to forget the terrible dead,
But shrieked when she saw the key was red,
And sickened and shook with an awful dread

When she heard Bluebeard was coming.
He did not appear to notice her pain;
But he took his keys, and seeing the stain,
He stopped in the middle of the refrain
    That he had been quietly humming.

"Mighty well, madam!" said he, "mighty well!
What does this little blood-stain tell?
You've broken your promise; prepare to dwell
    With the wives I've had before you!
You've broken your promise, and you shall die."
Then Fatima, supposing her death was nigh,
Fell on her knees and began to cry,
    "Have mercy, I implore you!"

"No!" shouted Bluebeard, drawing his sword;
"You shall die this very minute," he roared.
"Grant me time to prepare to meet my Lord,"
    The terrified woman entreated.
"Only ten minutes," he roared again;
And holding his watch by its great gold chain,
He marked on the dial the fatal ten,
    And retired till they were completed.

"Sister, oh, sister, fly up to the tower!
Look for release from this murderer's power!
Our brothers should be here this very hour;—
    Speak! Does there come assistance?"
"No: I see nothing but sheep on the hill."
"Look again, sister!" "I'm looking still,
But naught can I see, whether good or ill,
    Save a flurry of dust in the distance."

"Time's up!" shouted Bluebeard, out from his room.
"This moment shall witness your terrible doom,
And give you a dwelling within the room
    Whose secrets you have invaded."
"Comes there no help for my terrible need?"
"There are horsemen twain riding hither with speed."
"Oh! tell them to ride very fast indeed,
    Or I must meet death unaided."

"Time's fully up. Now have done with your prayer,"
Shouted Bluebeard, swinging his sword on the stair;
Then he entered, and grasping her beautiful hair,
   Swung his glittering weapon around him;
But a loud knock rang at the castle-gate,
And Fatima was saved from her horrible fate,
For, shocked with surprise, he paused too late;
   And then the two soldiers found him.

They were her brothers, and quick as they knew
What the fiend was doing, their swords they drew,
And attacked him fiercely, and ran him through,
   So that soon he was mortally wounded.
With a wild remorse was his conscience filled
When he thought of the hapless wives he had killed;
But quickly the last of his blood was spilled,
   And his dying groan was sounded.

As soon as Fatima recovered from fright,
She embraced her brothers with great delight;
And they were as glad and as grateful quite
   As she was glad and grateful.
Then they all went out, from that scene of pain,
And sought in quietude to regain
Their minds, which had come to be quite insane,
   In a place so horrid and hateful.

'Twas a private funeral Bluebeard had;
For the people knew he was very bad,
And, though they said nothing, they all were glad
   For the fall of the evil-doer;
But Fatima first ordered some graves to be made,
And there the unfortunate ladies were laid,
And after some painful months, with the aid
   Of her friends, her spirits came to her.

Then she cheered the hearts of the suffering poor,
And an acre of land around each door,
And a cow and a couple of sheep, or more,

To her tenantry she granted.
So all of them had enough to eat,
And their love for her was so complete
They would kiss the dust from her little feet,
    Or do any thing she wanted.

Samuel.

Capital! Capital! Wasn't it good!
    I should like to have been her brother!
If I had been one, you may guess there would
    Have been little work for the other.
I'd have run him right through the heart, just so!
And cut off his head at a single blow,
And killed him so quickly he'd never know
What it was that struck him, wouldn't I, Joe?

Joseph.

You are very brave with your bragging tongue;
But if you had been there, you'd have sung
    A very different tune.
Poor Bluebeard! He would have been afraid
Of a little boy with a penknife blade,
    Or a tiny pewter spoon!

Samuel.

It makes no difference what you say,
(Pretty little boy, afraid to play!)
But it served him rightly any way,
    And gave him just his due.
And wasn't it good that his little wife
Should live in his castle the rest of her life,
    And have all his money too?

Rebekah.

I'm thinking of the ladies who
Were lying in the Chamber Blue,
With all their small necks cut in two.

I see them lying, half a score,
In a long row upon the floor,
Their cold, white bosoms marked with gore.

I know the sweet Fatima would
Have put their heads on if she could;
And made them live—she was so good;

And washed their faces at the sink;
But Bluebeard was not sane, I think:
I wonder if he did not drink!

For no man in his proper mind
Would be so cruelly inclined
As to kill the ladies who were kind.

CITY AND COUNTRY.

MRS. E. B. P.

Characters.—JENNIE FLASH, *a City Girl.* MARY JONES, *a Country Girl.* MR. *and* MRS. FLASH. MR. *and* MRS. JONES.

SCENE—*A Parlor.* JENNIE, *dressed very finely, reclining languidly in an easy chair.* MARY, *dressed plainly, sitting at a table, taking flowers from a basket for two vases standing near.*

Jennie. How terribly tiresome it must be always to live in the country! I've hardly been here an hour, yet it seems like an age.

Mary. I'm sorry you find it so dull. Wouldn't you like to help me arrange these flowers?

Jennie. No, I thank you; it fatigues me to work.

Mary. Work! Why, this is nothing but play. I thought you would enjoy it. These are all wild flowers I gathered this morning in the woods.

Jennie. Mercy on me! You don't wander round in the woods *alone* after flowers—do you?

Mary. Yes, indeed. Why not, pray? You have no idea how pleasant it is; but you shall go with me to-morrow, if you like.

Jennie. O, no; not for the world. I should die of fright. The wild beasts and reptiles, you know.

Mary (*she laughs so heartily that she drops her flowers*). You must excuse me for laughing; but the idea of wild beasts in our wood-lot is so amusing! We should certainly see nothing more ferocious than a gray squirrel, or perhaps a rabbit. And as for reptiles—well, to be sure, I did kill three snakes this morning—two green ones and a stripped one; but they were harmless little things; and I don't know what I did it for, unless it's because I've got into the habit of killing all the snakes I see.

Jennie (*fanning herself violently*). How horrid! Killing snakes! It makes me sick to think of it. I should faint away at the bare sight of one.

Mary. O, no; I hope not. See what a lovely bird's egg I found. (*takes one from the basket*) It was in a nest almost at the top of a pine tree. Some birds like pines better than any other tree to build in. I was determined, when I saw the nest, to add to my collection.

Jennie (*clasping her hands in horror*). Climb a tree!

Mary (*smiling*). Yes, indeed; it's fine sport, I assure you. I will teach you while you are here.

Jennie. No, I thank you; I have no ambition to learn such unladylike sport.

Mary. How sorry I am! Look at these rose-colored flowers. (*passing them to her*) Brother Johnny and I used to call them "Whip-poor-will's shoes," when we were little. Is it not beautiful?

Jennie. Very pretty. You admire these wild flowers so much, I don't know what you *would* think if you were to go into our garden. We have a greater variety of rare plants and flowers than any one near us.

Mary. You find a great deal of pleasure in cultivating them, no doubt.

Jennie. I seldom go into the garden. Mamma and the gardener attend to that. I should burn and tan, and look frightfully countrified, if I did. And then too, I have no time.

Mary. Indeed, you are very industrious.

Jennie. O, no, I am not; but I attend so many parties that it is usually very late when I rise. Then, I practise a long time every day. I suppose you have never seen a piano. I have an elegant

Steinway rose-wood, with pearl keys. I preferred the keys pearl, my hands are so delicate. (*looking at them and then at* MARY's.)

Mary. Well, mine are brown enough; but I flatter myself they are useful hands, for they have got well tanned this summer helping father rake and load hay.

Jennie. How very strong and healthy you are! All country people are so, I believe. I should not care to be so, it is so vulgar, you know.

Mary. That is just as one thinks. (*voices approaching.* MARY *rises and opens the door.*)

MR. JONES *and* MR. FLASH *enter.*

You have got home, father, at last. This is Miss Jennie Flash.

Mr. Jones (*shaking hands with her*). Well, well, well! I want to know if this is the Mary Jane that I have seen so many times making mud pies when you lived down in Pumpkin Valley. I declare, friend Flash, I never should have guessed this fine young lady and that little girl, with brown freckles all over her nose, were the same.

MRS. JONES *and* MRS. FLASH *enter.*

Well, mother, what do you think? this is friend Flash's daughter. Jennie, they call her now, I believe.

Mrs. Jones (*takes her hand and kisses her*). I want to know. And this is really that little barefooted girl that I used to see playing round out doors? I can hardly realize it. But then, "fine feathers make fine birds"—don't they, my dear?

Mr. Jones. Ah yes; that's t. That oil speculation of yours was a lucky thing, friend Flash.

Mr. Flash. I don't know about that. Wife and I have about concluded that it was a most unlucky "strike," it has made such a *very* fine lady of our little girl here. We are almost afraid that she won't know her father and mother soon.

Mrs. Jones. O, not so bad as that. You are going to leave her here, and we will get all those foolish fine notions out of her in a little while.

Jennie. I didn't know you were ashamed of me, papa. I'm sure you spent enough on my education.

Mr. Flash. Too much, too much, my dear. You have lost your roses, and I have lost my little freckled, barefooted girl that made such nice mud pies. If you were only plump and fresh, like Mary here, what a proud father I should be!

Jennie. Well, papa, I do think you have retained some very vulgar tastes, with all your wealth. But I see that no one cares anything about style, and grace, and the Grecian bend, here in the country. To be thought anything of, a young lady must be freckled, and climb trees, and rake hay. All my city friends would cut my acquaintance.

Mrs. Flash. Don't quarrel with your father, dear. He is older than you are, and knows just what a good and true woman should be.

Mr. Jones. No, no, no; don't tease the little lady; just let her alone, and she will come round to our side herself in a week or two. Let her alone. That's the way I do with my ducks and chickens, and they allurs come out all right. Come, Mary; give us a song, and that will brighten us up again. (MARY *goes to a piano, which a screen had concealed.* JENNIE *performs pantomimic gestures of surprise and shame, and goes and seats herself beside her father, leaning her head against his shoulder. Curtain falls at close of song.*)

MAINE (Acting Charade).

M. B. C. SLADE.

A little girl with long curls enters, tossing her hair and running across the stage as she recites her couplet.

THE WORD, MANE (*Maine*).

Girl. If I were a colt I should toss it so,
    As I cantered along the shore.

THE WORD, MAIN (*Maine*).

Boy. If I were a sailor boy o'er it I'd go,
And for months not come back any more.

Both (*in concert*). 'Tis the farthest first of a glorious number,
And like an old garret, is *full of lumber*.
We'll help you by saying it is a State,
And now for your answer you see us wait.

Girl. Now, while you are guessing, I'll *make it plain;*
For, do you see, I am making MAINE ?

At the closing couplet the little girl draws the outlines of Maine rapidly upon the board.

NATURE'S HEROES.

CHARACTERS.

CARATACH, General of the Britons.
HENGO, a brave boy, nephew to Caratach.
MACER, a Roman Officer.
JUDAS, a cowardly Roman Corporal.
ROMAN SOLDIERS, two or more.

INTRODUCTORY.

The following stirring and affecting scenes are from the *Bonduca* of *Beaumont* and *Fletcher*. They present fine illustrations of the heroic temper displayed by CARATACH, King of Britain, and his nephew, HENGO, when driven to bay by the invading Romans. The time in which the action is supposed to take place is in the first century of the Christian era. The two Britons can be attired somewhat like Scottish Highlanders, with short cloaks instead of plaids ; the three Romans as seen in pictures of Julius Cæsar's legions. Of course scenery and special costumes may be dispensed with, where the performance takes place in parlors and other places unfitted for theatrical display.

SCENE I.—*A Forest.*

Enter CARATACH *and* HENGO. *They pause at* C.

Caratach. How does my boy ?
Hengo. I do not fear.

Car. My good boy?
Hengo. I know, uncle,
  We must all die; my little brother died,
  I saw him die, and he died smiling; sure,
  There's no great pain in't, uncle. But pray tell me
  Whither must we go when we're dead?
Car. Strange questions!
  Why, to the blessed'st place, boy. Ever sweetness
  And happiness dwell there.
Hengo. Will you come to me?
Car. Yes, my sweet boy.
Hengo. Mine aunt, too, and my cousins?
Car. All, my good child.
Hengo. No Romans, uncle?
Car. No, boy.
Hengo. I should be loath to meet them there.
Car. No ill men,
  That live by violence and strong oppression,
  Come thither; 'tis for those the gods love, good men.
Hengo. Why, then, I care not when I go, for surely
  I am persuaded they love me; I never
  Blasphemed them, uncle; nor transgressed my parents;
  I always said my prayers.
Car. Thou shalt go, then,
  Indeed thou shalt.
Hengo. When they please.
Car. That's my good boy!
  Art thou not weary, Hengo?
Hengo. Weary, uncle?
  I've heard you say you've marched all day in armor.
Car. I have, boy.
Hengo. Am not I your kinsman?
Car. Yes.
Hengo. And am not I as fully allied unto you
  In those brave things as blood?
Car. Thou art too tender.
Hengo. To go upon my legs? They were made to bear me.
  I can play twenty miles a day; I see no reason,

But to preserve my country and myself,
I should march forty.

Car. What wouldst thou be, living
To wear a man's strength!

Hengo. Why, a Caratach, (*with fire*)
A Roman-hater, a scourge sent from heaven
To whip these proud thieves, from our kingdom. Hark!
(*drum*)
Hark, uncle, hark! I hear a drum.

Enter at L. JUDAS *and soldiers.* CARATACH *retires to* R., *shielding* HENGO, *and sternly eyeing soldiers.*

Judas. Beat softly;
Softly, I say; they're here. Who dares charge?

First Sol. He
That dares be knocked o' the head;
I'll not come near him.

Judas. Retire again, and watch, then How he stares!
He has eyes would kill a dragon.
Mark the boy well;
If we could take or kill him. A curse on ye,
How fierce ye look! See how he broods the boy!
The devil dwells in's scabbard. Back, I say!
Apace, apace! he has found us. (*they retire.*)

Car. Do ye hunt us?

Hengo. Uncle, good uncle, see! the thin, starved rascal,
The eating Roman, see where he thrids the thickets;
Kill him, dear uncle, kill him!

Car. Do ye make us foxes?—
Here, hold my charging-staff, and keep the place, boy!
I am at bay, and, like a bull, I'll bear me.
Stand, stand, ye rogues, ye squirrels! (*draws and rushes after them,* L.)

Hengo. Now he pays them;
Oh, that I had a man's strength!

Enter at L. JUDAS.

Judas. Here's the boy;
　　Mine own, I thank my fortune.
Hengo. Uncle, uncle!
　　Famine is fallen upon me, uncle.
Judas. Come, sir,
　　Yield willingly; your uncle's out of hearing.
Hengo. I defy thee,
　　Thou mock-made man of mat. Charge home, sirrah!
　　Hang thee, base slave, thou shak'st.
Judas. Upon my conscience,
　　The boy will beat me! how it looks, how bravely,
　　How confident the worm is! a scabbed boy
　　To handle me thus! Yield, or I cut thy head off.
Hengo. Thou darest not cut my finger; here 'tis, touch it.
Judas. The boy speaks sword and buckler! Pr'ythee yield, boy;
　　Come, here's an apple; yield.
Hengo (aside). By Heaven, he fears me!
　　I'll give you sharper language. When, ye coward,
　　When come ye up?
Judas. If he should beat me——
Hengo. When, sir?
　　I long to kill thee! Come, thou
　　Canst not 'scape me;
　　I've twenty ways to charge thee, twenty deaths
　　Attend my bloody staff.
Judas. Sure, 'tis the devil,
　　A dwarf devil in a doublet!
Hengo. I have killed
　　A captain, sirrah, a brave captain, and when I've done,
　　I've kicked him thus. Look here; see how I charge
　　This staff! (*threatens to charge.*)
Judas. Most certain this boy will cut my throat yet.

　　Enter, R., *two* Soldiers, *running. They rush past* Hengo.

First Sol. Flee, flee, he kills us.
Sec. Sol. He comes, he comes!

Judas. The devil take the hindmost!

(*Exeunt,* L., JUDAS *and soldiers.*)

Hengo. Run, run, ye rogues, ye precious rogues, ye rank rogues!
'A comes, 'a comes, 'a comes!' a comes! that's he, boys! (*goes to extreme* L.)
What a brave cry they make!

Enter CARATACH, R.

Car. How does my chicken?

Hengo. Faith, uncle, grown a soldier, a great soldier; (*meets* CARATACH *in* C.)
For, by the virtue of your charging-staff,
And a strange fighting face I put upon it,
I've out-braved Hunger.

Car. That's my boy, my sweet boy.
Come, chicken, let's go seek some place of strength
(The country's full of scouts) to rest awhile in;
Thou wilt not else be able to endure
The journey to my country. Fruits and water
Must be your food awhile, boy.

Hengo. Anything;
I can eat moss—nay, I can live on anger,
To vex these Romans. Let's be wary, uncle.

Car. I warrant thee; come cheerfully.

Hengo. And boldly. (*Exeunt,* L.)

SCENE II.—*Another part of the forest.*

Enter MACER *and* JUDAS, L.

Macer. What news?

Judas. I've lodged him; rouse him, he that dares.

Macer. Where, Judas?

Judas. On a steep rock i' th' woods, the boy, too, with him;
And there he swears he'll keep his Christmas, Macer,
But he will come away with full conditions,
Bravely, and like a Briton. He paid part of us;
Yet I think we fought bravely. For mine own part,

I was four several times at half-sword with him,
Twice stood his partizan; but the plain truth is,
He's a mere devil, and no man. I' th' end he swinged us,
And swinged us soundly, too; he fights by witchcraft;
Yet for all that I saw him lodged.

Macer. Take more men, and scout him round.
What victuals has he?

Judas. Not a piece of biscuit,
Not so much as will stop a tooth, nor water.
They lie
Just like a brace of bear-whelps, close and crafty,
Sucking their fingers for their food.
His sword by his side, plumbs of a pound weight by him,
Will make your chops ache. You'll find it more labor
To win him living than climbing of a crow's nest.

Macer. Away, and compass him; we shall come up,
I'm sure, within these two hours. Watch him close. (*Exit.*)

Judas. He shall fly through the air if he escape me.

Enter a SOLDIER *with meat and a bottle.*

Sol. Here, Judas, I have brought the meat and water.

Judas. Hang it on the side of the rock, as though the Britons
Stole hither to relieve him. Who first ventures
To fetch it off is ours. I cannot see him.

Sol. He lies close, in a hole above, I know it,
Gnawing upon his anger,—Ha! no; 'tis not he.

Judas. Make no noise; if he stirs, a deadly tempest
Of huge stones falls upon.

SOLDIER *goes out,* R., *leaves provisions behind scene, and returns to* JUDAS.

Sol. 'Tis done! Away, close! (*Exeunt.*)

SCENE II.—CARATACH *discovered, with* HENGO *sleeping on the ground.*

Car. Sleep still, sleep sweetly, child; 'tis all thou feed'st on.

No gentle Briton near, no valiant charity,
    To bring thee food? Poor knave, thou'rt sick, extreme
        sick,
Almost grown wild for meat; and yet thy goodness
Will not confess nor show it. All the woods
Are double lined with soldiers; no way left us
To make a noble 'scape. I'll sit down by thee,
And, when thou wak'st, either get meat to save thee,
Or lose my life i' th' purchase; good gods comfort thee.
The boy begins to stir; thy safety made,
Would my soul were in heaven.

Hengo (*waking*).   Oh, noble uncle,
    Look out; I dreamed we were betrayed.

Car.   No harm, boy;
    'Tis but thy emptiness that breeds these fancies;
    Thou shalt have meat anon.

Hengo.   A little, uncle,
    And I shall hold out bravely.

(HENGO *rises.* CARATACH *espies the meat and water outside.*)

Car.   Courage, my boy! I have found meat.
    Look, Hengo. (*joyously*)
    Look where some blessed Briton, to preserve thee,
    Has hung a little food and drink;
    Cheer up, boy;
    Do not forsake me now!

Hengo.   Oh, uncle, uncle,
    I feel I cannot stay long; yet I'll fetch it,
    To keep your noble life. Uncle, I'm heart-whole,
    And would live.

Car.   Thou shalt, long, I hope.

Hengo. But my head, uncle! Methinks the rock goes round.

Enter stealthily JUDAS, *with bow and arrow,* L.

    Do not you hear
    The noise of bells?

Car. Of bells, boy? 'Tis thy fancy.

Hengo.   Methinks, sir,
    They ring a strange sad knell, a preparation
    To some near funeral of state. Nay, weep not,
    Mine own sweet uncle! you will kill me sooner.
Car. Oh, my poor chicken!
Hengo.   Fie! faint-hearted uncle!
Car. I'll go myself, boy.
Hengo.   No, as you love me, uncle!
    I will not eat it if I do not fetch it.
    The danger only I desire. When I have brought it, uncle,
    We'll be as merry——
Car.   Go, i' th' name of Heaven, boy!
Hengo (*exit,* R.). I have it. (JUDAS *shoots*) Oh!
Car.   What ail'st thou?

    Re-enter HENGO, *with an arrow in his side.*

Hengo. Oh, my best uncle, I am slain!
Car. (*seeing* JUDAS).   I see you,
    And Heaven direct my hand! (JUDAS *steals off,* L. CARA-
    TACH *hurls a stone after him*) Destruction
    Go with thy coward soul! How dost thou, boy? (*supports*
    HENGO.)
Hengo. Oh, uncle, uncle,
    Oh, how it pricks me—am I preserved for this?—
    Extremely pricks me.
Car.   Coward, rascal, coward!
    Dogs eat thy flesh!
Hengo. Oh, I bleed hard; I faint too; out upon't,
    How sick I am!—The lean rogue, uncle!
Car.   Look, boy!
    I've laid him sure enough.
Hengo.   Have you knocked his brains out?
Car. I warrant thee, for stirring more. Cheer up, child.
Hengo. Hold my sides hard; stop, stop; oh, wretched fortune,
    Must we part thus? Still I grow sicker, uncle.
Car. Heaven look upon this noble child!
Hengo.   I once hoped

        I should have lived to have met these bloody Romans
At my sword's point, to have revenged my father,
To have beaten them. Oh, hold me hard! But, uncle——
Car. Thou shalt live still, I hope, boy. Shall I draw it?
Hengo. You draw away my soul, then; I would live
        A little longer—spare me, Heavens!—but only (*tries to stand alone*)
        To thank you for your tender love. Good uncle,
Good, noble uncle, weep not!
Car.   Oh, my chicken,
My dear boy, what shall I lose?
Hengo.   Why, a child,
That must have died, however; had this 'scaped me,
Fever or famine—I was born to die, sir.
Car. But thus unblown, my boy?
Hengo.   I go the straighter
My journey to the gods. Sure I shall know you
When you come, uncle?
Car.   Yes, boy.
Hengo.   And I hope
We shall enjoy together that great blessedness
You told me of.
Car.   Most certain, child.
Hengo.   I grow cold;
Mine eyes are going.
Car.   Lift them up.
Hengo.   Pray for me;
And, noble uncle, when my bones are ashes,
Think of your little nephew. Mercy!
Car.   Mercy!
You blessed angels, take him.
Hengo.   Kiss me. So.
Farewell, farewell! (*dies.*)
Car.   Farewell the hopes of Britain!
Thou royal graft, farewell forever! Time and death
You've done your worst. Fortune, now see, now proudly
Pluck off thy veil, and view thy triumph. Look,
Look what thou hast brought this land to. Oh, fair flower,

How lovely yet thy ruins show, how sweetly
Even death embraces thee! The Peace of Heaven,
The fellowship of all great souls, be with thee! (*mournful music.*)   (*Curtain.*)

HARD TO SUIT ALL.

Characters.—SCHOOLMASTER; ISAAC, *a school-boy;* MR. FOSDICK; BILL, *his son;* MRS. O'CLARY, *Irish;* PATRICK, *her son;* ESQ. SNYDER; JONAS, *his son;* SAUNDERS, *drunken;* JABEZ, *his son; some half-dozen school-boys.*

Master (setting copies, alone). Well, so here I am again, after another night's sleep. But, sleep or no sleep, I feel about as much fatigued in the morning as I do at night. It is impossible to get the cares and anxieties of my profession out of my mind. It does seem to me that the parents of some of my pupils are very unfeeling; for I know I have done my very best to keep a good school—and, however I may have failed in some instances, I have the satisfaction of feeling, in my conscience, that my best endeavors have been devoted to my work. A merry lot of copies here, to be set before school-time. (*looking at his watch*) But "a diligent hand will accomplish much;" by the way, that will do for a copy for Jonas Snyder—little culprit! he was very idle yesterday. (*thinking and writing*) What can that story mean, which Mr. Truetell told me this morning? Five or six!—who could they be?—five or six of the parents of my scholars dreadfully offended! Let me see; what have I done? Nothing very lately, that I recollect. Let's see—yesterday? no, there was nothing yesterday, except that I detained the class in geography till they got their lessons. Oh, yes; Jonas Snyder was punished for idleness. But I spoke to him four or five times, and he would do nothing but whisper, and whittle his bench; and, when at last he half eat up an apple, and threw the rest at Jacob Readslow, I thought he deserved it. Let's see; I gave him six claps—three on each hand; well, he did not get more than his deserts.

Enter one of the scholars, with his books under his arm, walking slowly, and eyeing the master, to his seat. Master, still busy, and thinking, by and by says: Isaac, you may come to me.

Isaac (walks along, and says). Sir!

Master. Do you remember (*placing his pen over his ear, and turning earnestly and portentously round*) whether I punished any scholars yesterday?

Isaac. Yes, sir; you feruled Jone Snyder for playing and laughing.

Master. Did I punish any one else?

Isaac. Not as I recollect.

Master. Think, Isaac; think carefully.

Isaac. You kept a lot of us after school for not saying our lessons——

Master (quickly). You mean, Isaac, rather, I kept you to get your lessons, which you had neglected?

Isaac. Yes, sir; and you made Patrick O'Clary stop and sweep, because he stayed out too late after recess.

Master. Oh, yes! I remember that.

Isaac. He was as mad as a hop about it. He said he meant to tell his mother that you made him sweep for nothing.

Master. Hush! hush! You shouldn't tell tales! Do you remember any other punishments?

Isaac. No, sir; not yesterday. You hit Jabe Saunders a clip over the knuckles with the cowskin, day before yesterday;—don't you remember?—Just as he stretched out his hand to hook that old rag upon Tom Willis' collar, you came along behind him, and clip went the old whip right across his fingers, and down went the old rag. There, I never was more glad to see anything in my life! Little dirty, mean fellow!—he's always sticking things upon fellows. I saw him once pin an old dirty rag upon a man's coat, just as he was putting a letter into the post-office. I never saw such a fellow! (*the other boys coming in gradually, the master rings his little bell.*)

Master. Boys, come to order, and take your books. Now, boys, I wish to see if we can't have a good school to-day. Let's see; are we all here?

Boys. No sir! No sir!

Master. Who is absent?

Boys. Jone Snyder! Jabe Saunders! Patrick O'Clary! and——

Master. Speak one at a time, my boys. Don't make confusion, to begin with; and—(*looking around them*) oh! Bill Fosdick—only four!

One of the boys. Pat O'Clary is late. I saw him down in Baker-street, poking along! He always comes late——

Master. Did he say he was coming?

Same Boy. I asked him if he was coming to school, and he shook his head, and muttered out something about his mother, and I ran along and left him.

Master. Well, boys, now let us try to have a still school and close study to-day, and see if it is not more pleasant to learn than to play. (*rises and walks to and fro on the stage*) Take the geography lesson, James and Samuel, first thing this morning; and, Isaac, I don't wish to detain you again to-day. (*loud knock at the door.*)

Enter BILL FOSDICK, *walking importantly and consequentially up to the master.*

Bill. Here! father wants to see you at the door! (*master turns to go to the door, followed by* BILL, *who wishes to hear all that's said, and* MR. FOSDICK, *looking quite savage, steps right inside—the master politely bowing, with a "good-morning."*)

Fosdick. Here, sir; I want to see you about my boy! I don't like to have you keep him after school every day; I want him at home—and I should like to have you dismiss him when school is done. If he wants lickin', lick him—that's all; but don't you keep him here an hour or two every day after school—I don't send him here for that!

Master. But, my good sir, I have not often detained him; not more than twice within a fort——

Fos. Well, well, sir! don't you do it again!—that's all I have to say! If he behaves bad, you lick him—only do it in reason; but, when school is done, I want him dismissed!

Master. Sir, I do what I conceive to be my duty; and I serve all my scholars alike; and, while I would be willing to accommodate you, I shall do what I think is my duty. (*gathering spirit and gravity, and advancing*) Sir, do I understand you wish me to whip your son for not getting his lesson?

Fos. Yes—no—yes—in reason; I don't want my children's bones broke!

Master (*taking from the desk a cowhide*). Do you prefer your son should be whipped to being detained?

Fos. I don't think not getting his lessons is such a dreadful crime. I never used to get my lessons, and old Master Peppermint never used to lick me, and I am sure he never kept me after school; but we used to have schools good for sumfin in them days. Bill, go to your seat, and behave yourself! and, when school is done, you come home! That's all I have to say!

Master. But stop, my boy! (*speaking to* BILL, *decidedly*) There happen to be two sides to this question! There is something further to be said, before you go to your seat in this school.

Fos. What! you don't mean to turn him out of school, du ye? (*somebody knocks. A boy steps to the door, and in steps* MRS. O'CLARY, *who approaches* MR. FOSDICK.)

Mrs. O'Clary. Is it you that's the schoolmaster, sure? It's I that's after spaking to the schoolmaster. (*courtesying.*)

Fos. No; I'm no schoolmaster.

Master. What is your wish, madam?

Mrs. O'Clary. I wants to spake with the schoolmaster, I do, sir. (*courtesys.*)

Master. Well, madam, (*rapping to keep the boys still, who are disposed to laugh*) I am the schoolmaster. What is your wish?

Mrs. O'C. Why, sir, my little spalpeen of a son goes to this school, he does; and he says he's made to swape every day, he is; and it's all for nothing, he tills me; and sure I don't like it, I don't; and I'm kim to complain to ye, I have! It's Patrick O'Clary that I'm spaking of; and it's I that's his mither, I be; and his poor father was Paddy O'Clary from Cork, it was—rest his sowl!

Master. Well, madam, he has never swept but once, I believe; and that, surely, was not without a good reason.

Mrs. O'C. But himself tells a different story, he does; and I niver knew him till but one lie, in my life, I didn't; and that was as good as none. But the little spalpeen shall be after tilling his own story, he shall! for it's he that's waiting in the entry, and will till ye no lie, at all, at all—upon that ye may depind! though it's his mither that says it, and sure! (*calls*) Patrick! Patrick! come in, and till master how it's you that's kept to swape ivry day, and it's all for nothing, it is! Come in, I say, in a jiffy! (PATRICK, *scratching his head, enters*) Here's your mither, dear! now till your master—and till the truth—didn't ye till your mither that ye had to swape ivry day for nothing; and it's you that's going to be kept swaping ivry day for a month to come, and sure?

Master. Now tell the truth, Patrick.

Patrick (*looking at his mother*). No; I niver said no such words, and sure! I said how I's kept to swape yisterday, for staying out too late; and that's all I said 'bout it all, at all!

Mrs. O'C. "Cush la macree!" Little sonny, how you talk! He's frightened, he is, and sure! (*turning to* FOSDICK) He's always bashful, before company, he is. But, master, it's I that don't like to have him made to swape the school, indade; and, if you can do nothing else, I shall be in sad taking, I shall, and sure! If you should be after bating him, I should make no complaint. For I bates him myself, whiniver he lies to his mither—a little spalpeen that he is! But I can't bear to have him made to do the humbling work of swaping, at all, at all; and it's I that shall make a "clish ma claver," an' it's not stopped—indade I shall! (*somebody knocks.*)

Isaac (*steps to the door, and, returning, says :*). Esq. Snyder wishes to see you, sir.

Master (*smiling*). Well, ask Mr. Snyder to step in; we may as well have a regular court of it! (ISAAC *waits upon him in, leading* JONAS *with his hands poulticed.*)

Master (*smiling*). Good-morning, Mr. Snyder; walk in, sir!

Mr. Snyder (*rather gentlemanly*). I hope you will excuse my interrupting your school; but I called to inquire what Jonas, here, could have done, that you bruised him up at such a rate. Poor little fellow! he came home, taking on as if his heart would break! and both his hands swelled up bigger than mine! and he said you had been beating him for nothing! I thought I'd come up and inquire into it; for I don't hold to this banging and abusing children, and especially when they haven't done anything; though I'm a friend to good order.

Master. I was not aware that I punished him very severely, sir.

Mr. Snyder. Oh! it was dreadfully severe! Why, the poor little fellow's hands pained him so that his mother had to poultice them, and sit up with him all night! And this morning she wanted to come up to school with him herself; but I told her I guessed she better let me come. Jonas, do your hands ache now, dear?

Jonas (*holding them up together*). Oh! dreadfully! They feel as if they were in the fire!

Mr. Snyder. Well, dear, keep composed; don't cry, dear. Now sir, (*addressing the master*) this was all for nothing!

Master. No, sir! It was for something, I am thinking!

Jonas. I say I did not do nothing! so there, now! (*somebody knocks.*)

Master. Gentlemen, sit down. (*looking perplexed*) Sit down, madam. Give me a little time, and I'll endeavor to set the matter right. (*all sitting down but the boys.*)

Mr. Snyder. Why, I don't wish to make a serious matter of it. I shan't prosecute you. I was only going to ask if you couldn't devise some other kind of punishment than pommelling. If you'd make him stop after school, or set him to sweeping the house, or scouring the benches, or even whipped him with a cowhide or switchstick, I should not have complained; but I don't like this beating boys! (*knocking again.*)

Master. Isaac, go and see who is at the door. (ISAAC *goes, and in stalks* SAUNDERS *and his son* JABEZ.)

Saunders (*bowing and flourishing*). Here! hallo! Here, I say, Mr. Schoolmaster! settle up the score as ye goes along! I say, (*snatching a cowhide*) you have been horsewhipping my boy here, ha'n't you? By the fifteen gallon law! you don't come that game over the son of Nehemiah Saunders, you see! you pale-faced, good-for-nothing!——but pardon me, master; I ax your pardon; for 'Miah Saunders always was, and always will be, a gentleman! Ye see—don't ye see?—(*hiccoughing—lifts off the hat*)—ye see— I'll tell ye what, master, if I'd only known it yesterday, ye see,

I'd a been here and—but—ye see—yesterday—I was very particularly engaged; but now, (*approaching, and switching the cowhide*) ye see, we'll know who's the strongest! I'll give you——

Mrs. O'C. (*screeching*). La! what shall I do? If there's a going to be fighting, by St. Patrick, I shall go into hysterics! Oh dear! dear! dear!

Master. Oh! don't be frightened, madam.

Saunders (*looking at the woman*). Oh! ha! ha! Why, Cathleen O'Clary—ye see—why, have you left your wash-tubs to go to school? Why, bless my heart! Why, ye see, bless me!—the master here will have a most tractable pupil in you, Cathleen! Why, my stars! ye see—and here is my neighbor Fosdick! why, how de du, neighbor Fosdick? (*bowing very low to* SNYDER) How do you do, Esq. Snyder? Why, I hope I han't been disturbing a court, nor nothing! (*rubbing his head, etc.*) The truth is, I felt dreadfully provoked, when I heard that master here had been whipping my son with a rawhide, like a horse; and says I, I don't sleep till I have whipped him—and all for nothing, too! I've nothing against licking, Mr. Schoolmaster, if you use the right kind of licking. Ferule a boy, or give him a stick, till he cries "Enough!" but none of your horsewhipping, I say!—ye see—I can't stand that! (*during this speech,* JABE *archly hangs an old rag upon his father's coat, and steps back, and laughs at it.*)

Mr. Fosdick (*who saw it*). Mr. Saunders, what is that you've got upon your coat? (*examining.*)

Saunders. On my coat?—where? (*looks, and after a while finds it, and says, in awful rage*) Who did that?

Fos. It was your hopeful son, there.

Saunders. You little villain of a scamp! (*attempting to hit him with the whip, but staggering, falls*) I'll whip the hide all off you, I will! Master, he's in your house; order him to me, and I'll show you how to use the cowhide!

Master. Be calm, sir; be calm. Will you be good enough to sit down? You are a gentleman, you say; then oblige me by sitting down between these two gentlemen.

Saunders. That I will. I'll oblige any gentleman. (*after many attempts, gets to the seat.*)

Master. And now, gentlemen, and, (*bowing*) madam, I think we may each of us begin to see the beauty of variety, especially in the matter of opinion. That you may all undestand the whole case, I will state, in a few words, the facts, as they actually occurred. Day before yesterday, our young friend Jabez (*pointing to him*) was playing his favorite trick of hanging his rag-signal upon a school-mate, after the fashion in which he has here so filially served his father, within a few minutes; and standing near him at the time, with my whip in hand, I could not resist the temptation to salute his mischievous knuckles with a well-directed stroke, which, however effectually it may have cut his own fingers and his father's sensibilities, it seems has not cut off his ruling propensity. Yesterday was emphatically a day of sinning on my part. Jonas Snyder, whose little hands have swelled to such enormous magnitude, for constant idleness was often reproved; and, after all this, when he threw a portion of an apple at a more industrious boy, thus disturbing many of those well-disposed boys, he was called and feruled, receiving six strokes—three on each hand—with the rule I now show you. Little Patrick O'Clary was required to sweep the school-room floor, for a strong instance of tardiness at recess; and this punishment was given, because I did not wish to inflict a severer one upon so small a lad. And last, this little fellow (*pointing to* BILL FOSDICK) was detained, in common with seven others, to learn a lesson which he neglected to learn at the proper time.

Such are the facts. And yet each of you has assured me that I have incurred your displeasure by using a punishment you disapprove, and "all for nothing." You have each one taken the trouble to come to this room, to render my task—already sufficiently perplexing—still more so, by giving parental support to childish complaints, and imparting your censure, in no measured terms, upon the instructor of your children. But this is a most interesting case. You all happen to be here together, and you thus give me the opportunity I have long wished, to show you your own inconsistencies.

It is easy to complain of your teacher; but perhaps either of you, in your wisdom, would find it not quite so easy to take my place and escape censure. How would either of you have got along in the present instance? Mr. Fosdick, who is displeased with detention after school, would have, according to his own recommendation, resorted to "licking," either with ferule or whip. In this case he would have incurred the censure of his friends, Esq. Snyder and Mr. Saunders. The "squire," in turn, would have raised the displeasure of both his friends, by resorting to his favorite mode of detaining and cowhiding. Mistress O'Clary would give the "spalpeens" a "bating," as she says, after her own peculiar fashion, with which the squire and Mr. Saunders could not have been overmuch pleased. And Mr. Saunders—aye, Mr. 'Miah Saunders—if we may judge from the exhibition he has just given us, would have displeased even himself by proving to be what he most of all things detests—a champion of the cowhide. But what is a little curious, as it appears, is that, while I have not carried out the favorite scheme of either one of you—which, we have already seen, would be objectionable to each of the others—but have adopted a variety of punishments, and the very variety which your own collective suffrage would fix upon, I have got myself equally deep into hot water; and the grand question is now, What shall I do? If I take the course taken by you collectively, the result is the same. I see no other way but to take my own course, performing conscientiously my duties, in their time and after their manners, and then to demand of you, and all others, the right of being sustained!

Saunders (*jumping up*). Them is my sentiments, exactly! Ye see—I say—ye see—you go ahead, and—ye see—whip that little rascal of mine—ye see—just as much as you've a mind to—(*turning to the squire, who is rising*) and you shall have this whip to do it with. (*handing it to the master.*)

Mr. Snyder. Well, gentlemen, my opinion is that we have been tried and condemned by our own testimony, and there is no appeal. My judgment approves the master; and hereafter I shall neither hear nor make any more complaints. Jonas, (*turning to* JONAS) my son, if the master is willing, you may go home and tell your mother to take off those poultices, and then do you come to school as you are told;* and, if I hear any more of your complaints, I will double the dose you may receive at school.

Mrs. O'C. And sure, master, the wife of Paddy O'Clary is not the woman to resist authority in the new country; and, bless your sowl, if yon'll make my little spalpeen but a good boy, it's I that will kindly remember the favor, though ye make him swape until next Christmas! Here, Patrick, down upon your little knees of your own, and crave the master's forgiveness; for it's not Cathleen O'Clary——

Master. No, madam; that I shall not allow. I ask no one to kneel to me. I shall only require that he correct his past faults, and obey me in future.

Mrs. O'C. It's an ungrateful child he would be, if ever again he should be after troubling so kind a master. St. Patrick bless ye! (*taking little* PAT *by the hand, they go out.*)

Fos. (*taking the master by the hand, pleasantly*). Sir, I hope I shall profit by this day's lesson. I have only to say, that I am perfectly satisfied we are all wrong; and that is, perhaps, the best assurance I can give you that I think you are right. That's all I have to say.

Saunders. Right! right! neighbor Fosdick. We are all—ye see—we are all come out on the wrong side this time; a'nt we, squire? I tell ye what, Mr. Schoolmaster—'Miah Saunders never is ashamed to back out (*suits the action, etc* when he's wrong! I says, I—ye see—'Miah Saunders is all for good order! Whip that boy of mine—ye see—as much as you please! I'll not complain again—ye see; whip him—says I—ye see—whip him, and I —tell ye—if 'Miah Saunders don't back ye up—then, ye see— may I be chosen president of—cold water society! (*Exeunt.*)

THE EXCITEMENT AT KETTLEVILLE.

EPES SARGENT.

Characters.—BODKINS, *late in the employ of Messrs. Flimsy and Gauze;* DITTO, *a Young Man about Town, famous in private theatricals;* TINCTURE, *a Man with a Diploma;* MOPER, *a disappointed Candidate;* PONDER, *a Man who thinks before he speaks;* TOMMY, *a Youthful Bill-sticker;* MISS HAVERWAY, *a Popular Young Lecturer.*

Enter BODKINS *and* DITTO, *right, and* TINCTURE, MOPER, *and* PONDER, *one after the other, from the opposite side.*

Bodkins. Well met, gentlemen, well met! We are all of one way of thinking, I presume, in regard to the business of to-night?

Ditto. I hope, gentlemen, that Kettleville will do her duty, and her whole duty, on this occasion.

Tincture. We must put a stop to this woman's rights movement, or it will put a stop to us. Action, heroic action, as we doctors say, is the only remedy. Now's the time.

Moper. How will you do it? That's the question. It can't be done.

Bodkins. Brother Moper, you are always looking on the dark side of things. Why can't it be done?

Moper. Because the women carry too many guns for us.

Bodkins. Guns? Guns? Does this little Miss Haverway carry a gun?

Moper. She doesn't carry anything else. That little morocco roll, or cylinder, in which she pretends to carry her lecture, is an air-gun,—a deadly weapon.

Bodkins. Possible? But that's a matter for the police to look into. Ha, ha! We are not to be intimidated, gentlemen,—eh? We are true Americans. No cowards among us,—eh? The blood of seventy-six does not,—does not——

Ditto. Stagnate in our veins.

Bodkins. Thank you, sir. Does not stagnate in our veins. Surely not in mine,—not in mine!

Ponder. May I be allowed to ask a question?

All. Certainly.

Ponder. What are we here for?

Bodkins. We are here, Mr. Ponder, to protest against allowing the town hall to be used to-night by one Miss Haverway for her lecture on woman's rights. I appeal to every young man in the land, ought it not to make our blood—our blood——

Ditto. Boil with indignation.

Bodkins. Thank you, sir. Boil with indignation, to see these attempts, on the part of certain audacious women, to oppress us, and take the bread out of our mouths, just as we are entering on our several careers?

Ditto. Gentlemen, what could be more—more—more—Excuse this burst of feeling. There *are* chords—Well, sir, go on.

Bodkins. Consider my own case, gentlemen. I had a snug situation in the store of Messrs. Flimsy and Gauze, the great dealers in muslins, laces, and such. An easy berth. All I had to do was to stand behind a counter and show the lady customers the newest styles of collars. All at once I am told that my services are not wanted. And, gentlemen, as if to add insult to injury, I am advised that the spade and the plough expect me,—me, with my delicate *physique*. Gentlemen, why were my services no longer required?

Ditto. Yes, why, gentlemen,—why,—why? If, gentlemen, one single reminiscence of Lexington and Bunker Hill lingers in your minds,—if—if—Excuse me. I was carried away by my feelings. Go on, Mr. Bodkins.

Bodkins. My dismissal was accompanied with the information that a young lady—a young lady—(*sarcastically*) had been selected to take my place.

Tincture and *Moper.* Shame! Shame! Too bad! Too bad!

Ditto. Atrocious! Yes, abominable!

Moper. I tell you we are all going to the *bad* just as fast as we can go. The world isn't the world it used to be.

Ditto. Gentlemen, there was a time when the whole business of making and trimming bonnets, and of making female dresses, was in the hands of men. Any reader of Shakespeare must be aware of this. That time must be revived. The case of my friend Bodkins calls for redress,—re-dress, gentlemen.

Tincture. Hear *me*, sir, and you will admit that *my* case still more eloquently cries—cries——

Ditto. Aloud for vengeance.

Tincture. Ay, that's it. I was, as you may be aware, bred a physician. My father, agent for the sale of Plantation Bitters, gave me a diploma. It hangs framed over my mantel-piece. You may see it, any of you, without charge. No sooner had I settled down in the flourishing village of Onward, no sooner had I begun to physic and bleed the enterprising inhabitants, than a young woman calling herself a doctress—ha, ha! a doctress—made her appearance.

Ditto. Shame! Shame! Humbug, thy name is—woman!

Bodkins. There it is again! Woman! Always woman!

Moper. I tell you it's no use. We've got to come to it. We may as well be resigned, and put our noses peaceably down to the grindstone.

Ditto. Never! Never! No, by Saint Bride of Bothwell, no! False Douglas, thou hast lied.

Moper. You'll see, sir,—you'll see. Gentlemen, I can relate a still more exasperating case. The humble individual who addresses you studied for the ministry. I was a candidate to fill the pulpit in that same village of Onward. I had the reputation of being the most depressing preacher ever heard in those parts.

Ditto. Not poppy, nor mandragora, nor all the drowsy syrups of the East—Go on, sir, I was only musing aloud.

Moper. Everything looked encouraging. On one occasion, after I had preached, not a man, woman, or child of the congregation was seen to smile for a week. Everything, I say, looked encouraging, when, all at once——

Ditto. When all at once there appeared a woman!

Moper. You are right, sir; there appeared a woman. Will you believe it? The infatuated people of Onward have settled her over their first religious society. A woman!

Ditto. A female woman! Be ready, gods, with all your thunderbolts! Dash her in pieces! Must we endure all this?

Bodkins. Why, sir, in a degenerate city of degenerate New England, the city of Worcester——

Ditto. Three groans for Worcester!

Bodkins. They have actually elected women to serve on the school-committee.

Ditto. Enough! Enough! I have supped full of horrors.

Moper. O, that's nothing to what we shall have to swallow.

Ditto. Thus bad begins, but worse remains behind.

Bodkins. I had a brother——

Ditto. I had a brother once—a gentle boy.

Bodkins. Mine went into a printing-office to learn to set type. He hadn't been there a week when a girl was admitted; and now—now—just because she can set type twice as fast as any of the men, she is allowed equal wages.

Ditto. There it is again! The irrepressible woman! Why didn't they tear down the printing-office? Equal wages indeed!

Bodkins. Well, my brother, who is a brave little fellow, did the best thing he could: he helped snow-ball the girl, and succeeded in hitting her on the head with a piece of ice.

Ditto. He shall have a pension. Served her right. Equal wages indeed!

Tincture. And yet there are men—fiends, rather, in human shape, libels on their sex—who pretend to see no reason why women shouldn't be doctors, ministers, lawyers, architects, builders, merchants, manufacturers,—in short, whatever they please, or chance to have a faculty for.

Bodkins. See how they are crowding us men out of the paths of literature and art! Look at Mrs. Stowe! She is paid more for a single page than my friend Vivid, author of "The Beauty of Broadway," gets for a whole volume.

Tincture. Look at Rosa Bonheur, painter of beasts!

Ditto. Let's all go and have her take our likenesses.

Tincture. See her rolling in wealth, while my friend Daub, with a family to support, sees his splendid productions, so rich in all the colors of the rainbow, unsold in the auction-rooms!

Moper. What are we going to do about it? That's the question.

Ditto. Awake, arise, or be forever fallen.

Bodkins. And they are talking now of giving women the suffrage,—letting them vote.

Ditto. When that time comes, find me on Torno's cliff or Pambamarca's side

Ponder. May I be permitted to ask a question?

Bodkins. Certainly. We all go for free speech; that is, for free masculine speech.

Ponder. Aren't we all in favor of the principle of *no taxation without representation?* Answer me that.

All. Certainly. No doubt of it. Of course we are.

Ponder. Well, then, if women are taxed, ought they not——

Ditto. Gag him. Stop him. He has said enough.

Ponder. I say if women are taxed, ought they not——

Bodkins. Silence! We've had enough of that sort of talk.

Ditto. He's a woman's rights man. I thought as much. How like a fawning publican he looks!

Tincture. Kettleville is no place for you, sir.

Ditto. No, sir. Mount a velocipede and strike a bee-line for Worcester. That's your safe plan. Hence, horrible shadow! Unreal mockery, hence!

Moper. Gentlemen, strike but hear. You'd admit, I suppose, that women must live. What, then, would you have them do?

Bodkins. Do? Why, tend the children, and wash clothes.

Tincture. I don't know about that. I don't like to see our primary schools kept by young women, whilst there are so many deserving young men out of employment.

Ditto. That's the talk. And as for washing clothes, how many good, honest fellows are hard pushed, through the absurd custom of giving these jobs of washing and ironing to women!

Ponder. But, gentlemen, be reasonable. Women must live,—must have some means of support,—must——

Ditto. Tr-r-r-raitor to thy sex! Don't we come first? Are they not our born thralls? Are not we their natural lords and masters? Wretch, whom no sense of wrongs can rouse to vengeance!

Ponder. Really, Mr. Ditto, I am not accustomed to be treated in this most extraordinary, most vituperative, most ungentlemanly——

Bodkins. Peace, gentlemen! Let everything be harmonious, I beg you, on this occasion. We have met informally to consider the means of preventing the spread in Kettleville of these wild, heretical notions concerning women's rights, now so prevalent. Miss Haverway shall not lecture in Kettleville. Are we all agreed opon that?

Ditto. Are we all agreed?

Enter TOMMY, *a bill-poster.* TINCTURE *takes one of the bills.* TOMMY *prepares to paste up another.*

Tincture. Ha! What have we here? A poster! An announcement of the lecture. (*reads*) "The celebrated Miss Haverway, lecturer on woman's rights—" (*to* TOMMY) Youth, forbear!

Tommy. I'm not a youth, and I'll not forbear. Touch me, and I'll daub you with paste.

Bodkins. Boy, stop that, or you'll rue the day. We shall tear down that bill.

Tincture. Save your paste, youth, and vanish. (TOMMY *threatens then with his brush; they retreat.*)

Ditto. Punch him, jam him, down with him! He's nothing but an orphan, and there's no one to help him.

Moper. I think I may safely hit him with my cane.

As he draws near to strike, enter MISS HAVERWAY *with a cylindrical roll for papers in her hand.* MOPER, BODKINS, *and* TINCTURE, *show great alarm as she points it at them.*

Miss H. What's all this? Tommy, what's the matter?

Tommy. These fellows talk of pitching into me. I should like to see them do it, that's all.

Miss H. So would I.

Tommy. They threaten to tear down your poster.

Miss H. Do they? We'll see.

Tommy. I'll paste 'em all up against the wall, if you say so, miss.

Miss H. Leave them to me, Tommy, and proceed with your work.   (*Exit* TOMMY, *singing* "*O, I wish I was in Dixie.*")

Bodkins (aside). I don't quite like the looks of things.

Miss H. (approaching Bodkins). Well, sir, have you any objection to my bill? Have you any objection to *me*, sir?

Bodkins. My dear lady——

Miss H. Don't dear *me*, sir; and don't *lady* me, sir. Call me plain woman. (Bodkins, Tincture, *and* Moper *watch the roll in her hands, and manifest alarm when she points it at them.*)

Bodkins. Well, then, plain woman, I—I—I—that is, *we*—my friends here—Moper, Tincture, and the rest—not being quite able to see this matter of woman's rights in the light that you—your ladyship—I mean you plain woman—see it in——

Miss H. (explosively). And why not, sir? Why not, I should like to know? (Bodkins *gets behind* Tincture. Miss Haverway *paces the stage in an excited manner.*)

Tincture. We only thought, madam, there would be no harm in ventilating—that is, discussing—the points at issue, and so——

Miss H. (stopping suddenly before him). Points? Points? (*pointing the roll at him*) Tell me the truth. What have you been plotting? No evasion! (Bodkins *and* Tincture *get behind* Moper.)

Tincture (thrusting Moper *forward*). This gentleman, madam, will explain.

Moper. If you'll have the goodness, madam, just to lower the point of your air-gun—(*she thrusts the roll at* Moper, *and he retreats behind* Bodkins *and* Tincture.)

Miss H. (to Ditto). Well, sir—and you?

Ditto (laughing). I, Miss Haverway? In me behold your very humble servant. These gentlemen, conservative citizens of Kettleville, all except my friend Ponder here, I regret to say, have been making rare fools of themselves. They met for the preposterous purpose of devising some way of preventing you from lecturing this evening. To learn their plans, and, at the same time, to have some fun on my own account, I pretended to be one of the conspirators, and it is only now that I throw off the mask, and declare to them and to you that the booby who lifts a voice or a hand to prevent your lecturing as you propose will have to measure arms in set pugilistic encounter with your true knight to command, Mr. Frederick Ditto.

Miss H. Who says the days of chivalry are gone? Sir, I thank you.

Ditto. I have but one demand to make of these gentlemen, and that is, that they all attend your lecture. Mr. Ponder will come, I know.

Ponder. That was my intention from the first.

Miss H. (*to* BODKINS). You will come, sir? (*as he hesitates, she lifts her roll.*)

Bodkins. Really—O, yes, I'll come. Shall be most happy. (*examining her collar*) Real point lace, I declare!

Miss H. (*to* TINCTURE). And you, sir?

Tincture. Unless my patients——

Miss H. No excuse, sir.

Tincture. I will come. (*aside*) I wish I could prescribe for her just once.

Miss H. (*to* MOPER). You will follow their example, sir, of course.

Moper. Excuse me, but—(*seeing her roll levelled at him*) I will not fail, madam, to be present.

Miss H. I thought so.

Ditto. Allow me to escort you, Miss Haverway, to your hotel. Mr. Ponder, will you join us? (PONDER *bows assent.*)

(*As the three go off right,* MISS H. *turns, and goes toward the others with the roll extended, when* BODKINS, TINCTURE, *and* MOPER *go off abruptly left. Exeunt Omnes.*)

CONSIDER THE LILIES.

MARY B. C. SLADE.

The First Girl holds and shows a lily bulb. The Third shows leaves, stem and budding stalk. The Seventh a perfect crown of blossoms.

Class in concert. Consider—

First Girl. Let us consider them:
Just down below the stem,

                    Within the brown, warm ground,
                    The lily's bulb is found.
                    All winter long it slumbers so,
                    Beneath its covering of snow.

In Concert. *The lilies of the field ;—*

Second Girl. Along Judea's rills,
                    And o'er its fields and hills,
                    Grew scarlet lilies fair.
                    When Jesus saw them there,
                    From lilies of the field he drew
                    The lesson we shall bring to you.

In Concert. *How they grow :—*

Third Girl. Two little leaves, at first,
                    Must through the soft mold burst;
                    Next, tender, smooth and green,
                    The growing stem is seen;
                    And soon a tall, straight stalk is grown,
                    Where buds the lovely lily crown.

In Concert. *They toil not,—*

Fourth Girl. Ah, no, they never toil;
                    Fed by the moist, sweet soil,
                    Drinking the dews of night,
                    Nourished by sunbeams bright,
                    Fanned by the gentlest winds that blow,
                    In happy ease, the lilies grow.

In Concert. *Neither do they spin ;—*

Fifth Girl. The lilies spin? Not they!
                    Spiders and silk-worms may,
                    But lilies bloom for joy!
                    No cares their time employ.
                    Stem, leaf and bud and blossom bright,
                    Just grow for beauty and delight.

In Concert. *And yet I say unto you that even Solomon, in all his glory,—*

Sixth Girl.   To Solomon, the king,
                The people came, to bring
                Gold, and each precious gem,
                To deck his diadem.
                With scarlet and with purple shone
                The royal robes of Solomon.

In Concert. *Was not arrayed like one of these!—*

Seventh Girl.   Behold them now, and see,—
                Could kingly raiment be
                So beautiful, so rare,
                So gloriously fair?
                No human hand can learn the way
                Such tints of beauty to display.

In Concert. *Wherefore, if God clothe the grass of the field,—*

Eighth Girl.   Ah! 'tis the hand divine
                That makes the lilies shine!
                His rain, His dew, His light,
                Weave all their colors bright:
                I am so happy that I know
                'Tis God arrays the lilies so.

In Concert. *Will he not much more clothe you?—*

Ninth Girl.   Oh, yes! and so we must
                The lesson learn of trust.
                For lilies careth He?
                Much more His care for me!
                And this is why with joy we so
                Consider how the lilies grow.

BLUEBIRD AND ORIOLE.

[*For two girls.*]

Bluebird.   What swift, bright thing
            Is on the wing,

Singing out his soul?
'Tis the oriole
In colors bold,
All black and gold;
His deep nest swung
High boughs among
Of the tall elm's shade.

Oriole. Yes, I was made
Of a sunbright beam
In the dark shade's gleam.
My song is loud,
My flight is proud
To my queenly mate
As she swings in state.

Bluebird. Chirp, chirp, chiree!
Trill gay and free.
The sky is blue,
And the water too,
And I flit between
As blue, I ween,
While I dip and sing
On azure wing,
Golden Oriole!

Oriole. Your sweet trill and troll
On the ether float
From your fair blue throat;
But where's your nest
And your mate's gray breast?
Is it builded close
In the deep repose
Of a hollow tree?
Will you show it me?

Bluebird. In the linden shade,
Where a little maid

                Reared a tiny house,
                Broods my darling spouse.
                Sing low, sing sweet,
                By that blest retreat.
                We come and go
                With a song, you know,
                Sing low, sing low.

Both. Sing sweet, sing clear,
                High tide of the year!
                Love's tale is told
                By blue or gold,
                In cosy nests
                To brooding breasts.
                For hearts' delight
                All days are bright,
                While the eggs,—pale blue
                Or white,—break through,
                And the birdlings come
                For our waiting home!

THE CANDIDATE FOR CONGRESS.

Mr. Markman (walking alone in his counting-room). This is really quite an unexpected event—to be nominated for Congress. How surprised the old folks at home will be! Who would have thought that I, the poor counting-house clerk, would one day be sent to Congress. No doubt my wealth and standing as a merchant have induced the party to select me; for I have never been much engaged in political affairs, and am very far from being a demagogue. My friends, however, urge me to accept the nomination, saying that our party will fail if I do not. Well, if I am elected, I will do the best in my power; but there is the difficulty. Suppose I am defeated. What if I am, though? it is no disgrace. I will, however, use every honorable means not to be defeated.

Enter Mr. Puff.

(*aside*) One of the committee, I suppose. (*aloud*) I am happy to see you, sir. Pray be seated.

Mr. Puff (*speaking rapidly*.) Thank you, but can't stay—in a great hurry, you know. I am sent by the committee, to announce your nomination as our candidate for Congress. You have heard of it, no doubt, and are ready to join us.

Mr. Markman. I feel highly honored by the choice of our noble party, but have really had no time to reflect upon——

Mr. Puff. O, you must accept—your friends expect it. Our party will be ruined if you refuse.

Mr. Markman. That is a very poor reason for assuming such a great responsibility; but on the whole I have concluded to accept the nomination, and do the best in my power.

Mr. Puff. I am rejoiced to hear it, sir; allow me to congratulate you on this event. (*they shake hands.*)

Mr. Markman. Thank you; but we have not yet gained our object. We may lose our election.

Mr. Puff. No, indeed, we must not lose it—we shall not lose it; every wire must be pulled. That is my object in calling upon you this evening. I am to make a great speech in your favor to-morrow night, at the Hall; and I wish to ascertain some facts in relation to your private history, that I may rouse up the people in your behalf.

Mr. Markman (*laughing*). Ha, ha! Upon my word, Mr. Puff, I think the wisest way will be to say nothing about me; for very little can be said in praise of a quiet merchant like me, except, indeed, that I have always paid my debts.

Mr. Puff. Oh! that wouldn't be a circumstance. We must have something to shout about, or we shall lose the election. Were you ever a fireman?

Mr. Markman. Never in my life.

Mr. Puff. Did you ever save the life of some poor emigrant's child, by jumping into the water, or, in other words, the briny deep?

Mr. Markman. Never; for I never learned to swim.

Mr. Puff. Did you never save any body's life, in any manner?

Mr. Markman. Not to my knowledge; unless an occurrence last night be so called; but it is not worth mentioning.

Mr. Puff (*eagerly*). Let us hear it, by all means (*takes out a memorandum book and pencil.*)

Mr. Markman. I was riding home from from my office last night, through the darkness and rain, when the carriage suddenly stopped, and the coachman told me that a drunken man had fallen in the gutter, directly across the road. I ordered him to lift the man up, and call a policeman to take care of him. Had we left him there, he might have drowned; but any person would have done the same thing.

Mr. Puff. Never mind that, sir. It was done by your orders, and is a great credit to you. (*writes*) Friend of the poor; protects the unfortunate; raises the poor inebriate from the lowest depths of—of——

Mr. Markman. Of the gutter.

Mr. Puff. Of his degradation. That will make an excitement. But is there nothing warlike about you? Perhaps you were engaged in our glorious struggle for independence.

Mr. Markman. How could that be, as I was not born till long after that war?

Mr. Puff. Ah! true—I forgot. That's very unlucky. I should like to make a revolutionary hero of you. But, perhaps your father was in that war?

Mr. Markman. No; our family did come from England until the war closed.

Mr. Puff. What! were you British? How unfortunate! That will be against you.

Mr. Markman. Our family, like your own and many others, came from England; but how can that make any difference? We always liked the Americans, and sided with them—which was one reason why we came here.

Mr. Puff. That makes no difference. If your father came from England, it will prejudice the public somewhat against you.

Mr. Markman. Then the public is very unreasonable.

Mr. Puff. Yes; but it is very powerful, and we must respect its opinion. Can you not think of some relative who shared in the toil and danger of the Revolution?

Mr. Markman. My grandfather's cousin held the rank of sergeant among the militia.

Mr. Puff. That will do. (*writes*) Was he wounded?

Mr. Markman. I heard my grandfather say that his right heel was shattered by foolishly putting out his foot to stop a cannon-ball, which he supposed was nearly spent.

Mr. Puff. Good, good! Of course there is but one way of speaking of that circumstance; it is a remarkable historical fact. (*writes*) Your ancestry poured out their blood like water upon the ensanguined field of—of—what battle was it?

Mr. Markman. I really don't recollect.

Mr. Puff. Well, never mind—upon the ensanguined battle-field will do. Did you not engage in the last war? You surely must have been drafted to serve.

Mr. Markman. I was; but I hired a substitute.

Mr. Puff. All the same as though you went yourself. Was your substitute in any engagement?

Mr. Markman. I had the curiosity to make some inquiries about him, and found that he deserted the first time he heard the report of the enemy's musket, and——

Mr. Puff. Never mind about telling any further—he was in actual service; it will make a beautiful point in my speech. I wish he had taken a standard; it would produce a most thrilling effect to wave it over the heads of the people in the Hall.

Mr. Markman. I really wish he had taken one.

Mr. Puff. We have enough in the military line. I shall make a splendid speech. Good evening, sir; we shall soon be able to assure you of complete success (*they shake hands.*)

Mr. Markman. I cannot see what you have learned about me to-night to insure success. Pray do not exaggerate my virtues.

Mr. Puff. Oh! no fear of that. (*goes out.*)

Mr. Markman. What nonsense! I really dread the scene of confusion and intrigue that I must pass through; but I will preserve my own integrity through everything.

LITTLE RED RIDING-HOOD.

GEORGE COOPER.

Characters.—RED RIDING-HOOD; HER MOTHER; THE WOLF; FAIRY QUEEN; *Attendants.*

DRESSES.

RED RIDING-HOOD.—Scarlet cloak and hood.
HER MOTHER.—Old style woman's dress.
THE WOLF.—A buffalo robe, and animal's head, if possible.
FAIRY QUEEN and ATTENDANTS to be dressed in bright colors, as varied as possible. Wands, bearing silver and golden stars, made of pasteboard, are appropriate.

If necessary, a curtain may be dropped at the end of each scene. Where the scenery is scanty, imagination must make up the deficiency.

SCENE I.—*A Wood.*

Enter FAIRY QUEEN *and her attendants. The* QUEEN *takes her seat in the centre of the stage, and her attendants range themselves on each side.*

Attendants (in concert).

Hail, all hail our lovely queen!
Trip it lightly o'er the green!
Come from roses, dewy fair,
To her radiant court repair.
From the lily's swinging bell,
From the deep and ferny dell,
Trip it lightly o'er the green,
Hail, all hail our lovely queen!

Queen (rising and coming forward).

Good subjects, whom we call together here,
Unto our mandate every one give ear.
I know your loyalty is tried and true,
And for your aid this very hour I sue.
Know then, that in this forest, deep and wide,
A wicked wolf doth daily, nightly hide,—

Some truant fairy, from our band estranged,
And by my power to a monster changed.
To watch his steps, and guard from deadly harm
All mortals he may meet, be yours the charm.
Now, let me warn you, ere we speed away,
A little lady passes here to-day;
Red Riding-Hood, to many fays well known;
Watch o'er her while she treads these pathways lone.

Attendants (in concert).

Gentle queen, we all obey,
Near each mortal we will stay;
And our fairy watch we'll keep
When the world is hushed in sleep.
Naught shall harm the good of earth,
We will watch them from their birth;
Over sea and land we stray,—
Gentle queen, we all obey!

Queen.

Worthy subjects, fare you well!
  For the night is waning fast;
Weave round every heart your spell,
  Ere the lovely time be past.
Give to mortals pleasant dreams,
  Stay each tear-drop that would fall;
Till the morning's golden beams,
  Joy and beauty reign with all.

Attendants.

Gentle queen, we all obey. (*as before.*)
(*The* Queen *retires, followed by attendants.*)

SCENE II.—*A Room.*

Red Riding-Hood's *mother sewing at a table, and little* Red Riding-Hood *sitting at her feet.*

Mother.

My child, you've said your lessons perfect quite,
And all your sums are figured up all right.

Now, you may have a recess until noon;
The flowers are bright, the meadows are in tune.

Red Riding-Hood.

Thank you, mamma, but will you let me go
To grandmamma's, she's very sick, you know?
May I not take her something nice to eat,
Some luscious fruit, a pat of butter sweet?

Mother.

I'd like to have you go; but I'm afraid
You'll lose your way, o'er tangled hill and glade;
Then there are gipsies who might steal away
My little daughter, if alone she'd stray.

Red Riding-Hood.

Oh! no, mamma, I'll take the best of care
When in the woods, and shun all gipsies there.
To grandmamma's I'll gayly trot along,
And sing to birds and bees my merry song.

Mother.

Well, you may go; but *do* haste quickly back;
Should any harm befall,—alas! alack!
Your basket is all ready, pretty pet;
My warning I am sure you'll not forget.

Red Riding-Hood.

To do what you command, I'll always try,
So, mother dear, I bid you sweet good-bye.

RED RIDING-HOOD *puts on her bonnet, and takes up basket. She embraces her mother, kissing her repeatedly, and they depart in opposite directions.*

SCENE III.—*A Wood.*

Enter the WOLF, *growling.*

Wolf.

I've wandered up and down, but find no prey;
No delicate fat muttons hither stray.

These gloomy woods the pigs have e'en forsaken;
Should one pop in, I then might save my bacon.
My claws are aching for some morsel nice,
Ten meals a day for me don't half suffice.
I'll growl a bar, your spirits to delight,
Tho' " bars " best known to me " bar " sleep at night.

 Prowling, howling, up and down,
  When the moon is in the sky;
 While asleep is all the town,
  Monarch of the woods am I.
 Nestled in the woolly fold,
  Tender lambs know when I'm near;
 E'en the shepherd's heart so bold
  Quakes and shakes with nightly fear!
 Laughing at each bolt and bar—
  I'm the king by night, ha! ha!

 Creeping, sleeping, out of sight,
  In the forest deep and lone,
 Unto me the day is night;
  All these regions round I own.
 When the sun has gone to rest,
  Then my lips with joy I smack;
 Silver moonlight I love best,
  Dainty fare I never lack!
 Laughing at each bolt and bar—
  I'm the king by night, ha! ha!

Hark! I think I hear a footfall near;
I'll just withdraw until it doth appear.
My coat if seen would make folks turn aside,
I'll go this way, and hide my ragged hide.
     (*retires up stage.*)

  Enter RED RIDING-HOOD.

  Red Riding-Hood.
Oh, my! I'm wearied out, I do declare;
The sun is high—I must be almost there.

I hope I haven't missed my way; indeed,
These feet of mine must put on greater speed.

Wolf (aside).

A little girl! and rosy, fresh and nice!
I'll speak to her, and eat her in a trice!

Red Riding-Hood.

Oh, dear! I thought I heard somebody speak!
I'll wander on, my granny's cot to seek!

Wolf (coming forward).

Good morning, little girl! don't haste away;
Come here to me; why in such hurry, pray?

Red Riding-Hood.

Good day, Sir Wolf; I'm going to grandmamma's;
I had to foot it, for I missed the cars.

Wolf.

You're going to granny's, hey; what is your name?

Red Riding-Hood.

"Red Riding-Hood," I'm called,—are you quite tame?

Wolf.

As gentle as a lamb! *(aside)* The pretty crieter!
I really haven't got the heart to eat her!

Red Riding-Hood.

Well, I must go, for I must be back soon,
My ma expects me to return by noon.

Wolf.

Where does your granny live, my little dear?

Red Riding-Hood.

(aside) He's very civil, tho' his voice is queer!
Where does she live? about a mile from here.

Wolf.

Well, good-bye, for I won't detain;
I hope we both, some day, shall meet again.

Red Riding-Hood.

Good-by! (*aside*) I think the fellow's quite polite.
There is the cottage yonder, just in sight.   (*Exit.*)

Wolf.

But I'll these woods and marshes hurry thro',
And get to granny's house before you do!
Although there is a river to be met,
What do I care? My appetite 'twill whet!
"Laughing at each bolt and bar,—
I'm a king by night, ha! ha!"   (*Exit.*)

Enter the FAIRY QUEEN *and her attendants.*

Queen.

'Twas here I heard their voices; so away!
Some thro' the woods, some o'er the marshes stray.
To that sweet fay who does our bidding best,
We promise evermore delightful rest.

Fairies.

Swift as the silver lightning we are gone!
        (*Exeunt Fairies.*)

Queen.

Do as I bid; I'll follow you anon.
    Oh, I am a fairy queen;
My throne is the greenwood fair;
    I follow the birds and bees,
I sail thro' the wand'ring air.
    My heart has no care nor pain,
For these only mortals know;
    I sleep in the lily's breast,
I live in the summer's glow.

My days are a lovely dream,
    My nights are a sweet delight;
I dance on the moonlit sward;
    My sceptre is one of might.
I watch o'er each mortal need,
    And charm away weary care;
Wherever I gayly roam,
    No life is so sweet and fair!   (*Exit.*)

SCENE IV.—*A Room.*

The Wolf *is discovered in bed.*

Wolf.

I've eaten up the granny that was here,
A tough old soldier, quite a " granny dear."
So now, you see, I'm in the proper mood
To finish up with nice Red Riding-Hood. (*knock at the door*)
Hush! I must imitate the feeble voice
Of grandmamma, for that's my only choice. (*imitation*)
Who's that so early knocking at the door?

Red Riding-Hood (*outside*).

It's I, dear granny, and I've got a store
Of cakes and fruit, and such a dainty pat
Of butter mother sent you; think of that!

Wolf.

Come in, my darling, and we both shall sup;
Just pull the bobbin and the latch flies up.

Enter Red Riding-Hood.

Red Riding-Hood.

Good morning, granny; why, you're still in bed!

Wolf.

Yes, dearie dear, I've such an aching head!
Do come and sit down by my side awhile,
And sing a song my troubles to beguile.
How is your mother, and the cow and chickens?
This strong east wind has played with me the dickens.

Red Riding-Hood (*seated by the bed*).

What shall I sing you? tell me, granny dear.

Wolf.

Oh, anything my rheumatiz to cheer!

Red Riding-Hood (*sings.* Air—"*Viva la Compagnie*").

There was a wee chicken, just out of the shell—
Chickery, chickery, chick!
Along with her mother this chicken did dwell—
Chickery, chickery, chick!

That good lady told her by night or by day
That far from her home she must nevermore stray;
The daughter then promised that she would obey—
    Chickery, chickery, chick!

One morn, when the mother was out of her sight—
    Chickery, chickery, chick!
This daughter went out in the greatest delight—
    Chickery, chickery, chick!
She wandered along till she came to a brook,
Quite proud at her face in the water to look;
But there sat a frog in a green mossy nook—
    Chickery, chickery, chick!

"Oh! you're such a beauty!" the froggie then said,—
    Chickery, chickery, chick!
This flattered her so that it quite turned her head,—
    Chickery, chickery, chick!
"You're queen of the birds, and should wear a gold crown!"
Said sly little froggie, "pray on me don't frown!"
She dropped in the brook, and sank down, derry down!
    Chickery, chickery, chick!

Wolf.

You see, my sweet, the chicken got in danger
Because from home she liked to be a ranger.

Red Riding-Hood.

But, granny love, the fact to me appears,
That you have got two such tremendous ears!

Wolf.

They're better far for hearing, don't you see?
They're necessary for a dame like me.

Red Riding-Hood.

But, granny love, what staring eyes you've got.
What are those good for? tell me, granny, what?

Wolf.

Why, they are best to see with, little one,—
How chitter-chatter goes my darling's tongue!

Red Riding-Hood.
Then what a voice you have! you mustn't scold:
Wolf.
I'm getting hoarse, I've caught a shocking cold!
Red Riding-Hood.
Why, granny, you have got such ugly claws!
Wolf.
The better these to do my daily " chores."
Red Riding-Hood.
Oh, granny! why your teeth are long and white!
Wolf.
The better, girl, to eat with: you I'll bite!

The WOLF *rises and springs at* RED RIDING-HOOD, *who screams and kneels imploringly. Enter the* FAIRY QUEEN *and her attendants. The* WOLF *crouches in alarm.*

Fairy Queen.
Hold, monster! back unto your woodland den!
Within the darkest cave your limbs we'll pen!
What! would you this bright innocent devour?
Know we have watched her from her birthday hour.
With her dear blood would you your hands imbrue?
If she were killed what would the children do?
Away! nor let your ugly face be seen!
Go hide your head far from these meadows green.

Wolf.
I go, fair Queen, in manner most emphatic;
Thus easy to escape is most ecstatic!
(*Growls and exits.*)

Queen (*to* RED RIDING-HOOD, *who rises*).
Arise, sweet girl, whom we have saved from harm;
Still round thy way we weave our mighty charm.
Still may thy mem'ry live in glowing story,
Thy name still be each child's delight and glory.
With dance and song, we'll bear thee to thy home,
Then to the hills and valleys we must roam.

Thus may all fairies use each varied charm
To shield the good and innocent from harm!

Attendants (*in concert*).
Follow, follow, in delight,
When the earth is silver bright!
Wander to the moon afar,—
Look in every golden star!
Rock the birdies in their nest,
Chase the sun adown the west.
Dance our merry roundelay,—
Fairy sisters, now away!   (*Exeunt.*)

AGILITY (Dickens Charade).

G. B. BARTLETT.

SCENE I.

LITTLE NELL, *short calico dress, apron, rustic hat.*
GRANDFATHER, *powdered hair, ragged coat, knee-breeches, old white hat, cane.*

GRANDFATHER, *enters, leaning on* NELL'S *shoulder with his left hand, and on a cane with his right.*

Nell. We have nothing to fear now, dear grandfather.

G. Nothing to fear! Nothing to fear! If they took me from thee! Nobody is true to me. No, not one. Not even Nell.

Nell. Oh, do not say that, for if ever any one was true at heart, I am sure you know I am.

G. Then how can you bear to think we are safe, when they are searching for me everywhere?

Nell. Because I am sure we have not been followed. Look around, and see how quiet and still it is; we are alone together, and may ramble where we like. Not safe! could I feel easy when any danger threatened you?

G. True, true; what noise was that?

Nell. Only a bird flying into the wood, and leading the way for us to follow. You remember that we said we would walk in woods and fields, and by the side of rivers, and how happy we would be;

but here, while the sun shines above our heads, and everything is bright and happy, we are sadly loitering here and losing time. See what a pleasant path. Come on, dear grandpa.

SCENE II.

SARAH GAMP, *enormous bonnet, old black dress, red shawl tied over shoulders.*

PATIENT, *covered with bed-clothes on a couch, his arms and head in rapid motion, tossing from side to side.*

MRS. GAMP *sits at a table at her supper, eating ravenously, especially of cucumbers, taking up the vinegar on the blade of her knife. After eating a while she says:*

What a blessed thing it is, living in a world, to be able to make sick people happy in their beds. I do not belive a finer cucumber was ever growed. I'm sure I never see one. (*she then clutches the patient's throat, and makes him swallow the medicine she pours down*) I almost forgot the piller, I declare. (*she pulls the pillow from under the patient's head, and puts it in her chair*) There now, he is comfortable as he can be, I am sure, and I'll try to make myself as much so as I can. (*she then goes to sleep and is suddenly awakened by a cry from the patient.*)

Mrs. G. Hold your tongue!

P. Don't drink so much; don't you see how the sparkling water sinks in the fountain?

Mrs. G. Sparkling, indeed. I'll have a sparkling cup of tea. Just you hold your tougue.

P. One—two—

Mrs. G. Buckle my shoe.

P. Three—four—

Mrs. G. Shut the door.

P. That makes 522 men all dressed alike. Do you see them?

Mrs. G. I see them; all numbered like hackney coaches, ain't they?

P. 528—529—530—Look here!

Mrs. G. What's the matter now?

P. They are coming, four abreast. What's that upon the arm of each?

Mrs. G S·piders, perhaps.

P. Crape! black crape! Why do they wear it outside?

Mrs. G. Would you have them weare it inside? Hold your noise!

SCENE III.

DOLLY VARDEN, *red skirt, bright chintz overdress, laced bodice, cap.*

SIM TAPPERTIT, *long, bright waistcoat, knee-breeches.*

JOE, *dark waistcoat, knee-breeches.*

SIM *and* JOE *at table, waiting for breakfast.* SIM *gets up, goes to glass.*

Sim. I tell yer, Joe, there never was a person yet who could stand my eye. I can bring down any one with one of my powerful glances. I have only to eye them over and they give in at once.

DOLLY *enters with tea-tray and they sit down.* SIM *twists his face into grotesque contortions, looking lovingly at* DOLLY.

Joe (stops eating and observes SIM). Why, what's the matter with the lad? Is he choking?

Sim. Who?

Joe. Who? why, you. What do you mean by making those horrible faces over your breakfast?

Sim. Faces are matters of taste, sir.

Joe. Don't be a fool, Sim.

Sim. Fools are matters of taste, sir.

Joe. Why, what's the matter, Dolly? you are making faces now. The girls are as bad as the boys, now-a-days.

Dolly. It is the tea.

Joe. Is that all? Put some more milk in it. (DOLLY *runs out laughing.*)

Joe. That girl seems bewitched this morning.

Sim. It is all the effect of my eye. I eyed her over; no girl can stand my eye.

SCENE IV.

MR. BUMBLE, *high-collared coat, with cape trimmed with red braid, cane, cocked hat, knee-breeches.*

MRS. CORNEY, *black dress, high cap, white apron, white kerchief.*

She sits at a small, round table with dishes on it, and holds a small, black tea-pot.

Mrs. C. Drat the pot! Stupid little thing, it only holds enough for one or two cups. What use is it to anybody but a poor, desolate widow like me? (*knock*) Oh, come in with you. Don't stay there letting the cold air in. What's amiss now?

Mr. B. Nothing, marm, nothing.

Mrs. C. Dear me; is that Mr. Bumble?

Mr. B. At your service, madam.

Mrs. C. Hard weather.

Mr. B. Hard, indeed, marm. It blows hard enough to cut one's ears off.

Mrs. C. Won't you stay and have a cup of tea?

Mr. B. Oh, thank you, Mrs. Corney, thank you.

Mrs. B. Sweet, Mr. Bumble?

Mr. B. Very sweet, indeed. Mrs. Corney, you have a cat, I see, and kittens too, I declare!

Mrs. C. Oh, yes. I'm so fond of them; they are so happy, so cheerful, they are quite companions for me.

Mr. B. Very nice animals, mum, and so domestic.

Mrs. C. Oh, yes; and so fond of their home, too.

Mr. B. The cat or the kitten that could live in the house with you, Mrs. Corney, and not be fond of its home, must be an ass, madam.

Mrs. C. Oh, Mr. Bumble!

Mr. B. Yes, it would, and I'd drown it myself with pleasure.

Mrs. C. Then you are a cruel man, and very hard-hearted, beside.

Mr. B. Hard-hearted! Mrs. Corney, are you hard-hearted?

Mrs. C. What a curious question from a single man! What can you want to know for?

Mr. B. Don't tremble, my dear Mrs. Corney. What's the matter?

Mrs. C. Oh, nothing. Only I'm a poor, foolish, weak creetur.

Mr. B. Are you a weak creetur, Mrs. Corney?

Mrs. C. We are all weak creeturs.

Mr. B. So we are, so we are. This is a very nice apartment, Mrs. Corney. With one more added to it, it would be complete.

Mrs. C. It would be too much for one, Mr. Bumble.

Mr. B. But not too much for two, Mrs. Corney. Does the board furnish you with coals, Mrs. Corney?

Mrs. C. And candles!

Mr. B. Coals, candles, and house rent free! Oh, Mrs. Corney, what an angel you are. Compose your feelings, my dear Mrs. Corney, to say the little—little—word yes! One word more, my blessed angel, when shall it be?

Mrs. C. Whenever you please, you irresistible duck!

SCENE V.—*The whole word of the Charade.*

The Savage and the Maiden, from Nicholas Nickleby, to be acted in pantomime.

The Maiden *wears a short tarleton dress, covered with gold paper, and a wreath of paper roses.*

The Savage, *a red flannel skirt and bands over his shoulders made of red flannel trimmed with many-colored carpet yarns, leggins and cap of the same.*

The savage, becoming ferocious, makes a slide toward the maiden; but she avoids him in six twirls, and comes down at end of the last one upon the points of her toes. The savage relents and strokes his face with his right thumb as if struck with admiration for the beauty of the maiden. He thumps his chest and seems desperately in love. The maiden falls asleep on a sloping bank, and the savage leans his left ear on his left hand and nods. He then dances alone; the maiden wakes, rubs her eyes and also dances alone; the savage looking on in delight. After which he hands her a rose, which she at first refuses, and then accepts. The savage jumps for joy, the maiden follows suit, and both dance violently together, and finally he drops on one knee and the maiden stands on one foot upon his other knee.

SEVEN.

[For seven little girls and the class.]

1. Strike ends of the fingers upon the desk. 2. Point to the heavens. 3. Move right hand in an arch from right to left. 4. Clasp hands.

> One, two, three, four, five, six, seven! 1
> Count the lovely arch of heaven.2
> Seven bright colors make the bow,3
> Brightest, fairest things I know,2
> See the rainbow in the heaven! 2
> One, two, three, four, five, six seven! 1

Concert Recitation.—And God said, I do set my bow in the cloud.—Gen. ix. 13.

> One, two, three, four, five, six, seven! 1
> Hear the promise God hath given.4
> Seven troubles I may see,
> But the Lord will care for me!
> Hear the promise he hath given:
> One, two, three, four, five, six, seven! 1

Concert Recitation.—He shall deliver thee in six troubles; yea, in seven there shall no evil touch thee.—Job v. 19.

> One, two, three, four, five, six, seven! 1
> Nightly go across the heaven,3
> Seven bright stars, the Pleiades ;2
> And the Lord created these,4
> Nightly go across the heaven,3
> One, two, three, four, five, six, seven! 1

Concert Recitation.—Seek Him that maketh the seven stars, and Orion. The Lord is His name.—Amos v. 8.

> One, two, three, four, five, six, seven! 1
> Hear the rule by Jesus given;3
> Law of kindness, teaching me
> That forgiving I must be.
> Hear the rule by Jesus given,2
> One, two, three, four, five, six, seven.1

Concert Recitation.—If thy brother trespass against thee seven times in a day, and seven times in a day turn again to thee saying, I repent; thou shalt forgive him.—Luke xvii. 4.

LOVE OF COUNTRY.

[*For three boys*, JOHN, JAMES *and* HENRY.]

John. I have been thinking, boys, what a glorious thing it is to lay down one's life for the flag.

James. Why, you are in a patriotic mood this morning.

Henry. A glorious thing indeed! Look at young Charles Stanford, who came home from the war with one leg and an arm. Who cares for him now?

John. Who cares for him? Has he not the consciousness of knowing that he offered his life in the defence of the nation?

James. Yes, and what has his country done for him in return for what he sacrificed?

Henry. I think all this talk about the flag and the nation bosh!

John. Bosh! I am ashamed of you! Whose heart does not leap up at the sight of our national emblem streaming in triumph up in yonder sky? Go ask the wanderer in a foreign land how he feels to see his native flag floating from the mast of some good ship. Bosh, indeed!

James. Why, you would make an excellent stump-speaker.

Henry. I'd rather stay at home, and not run the risk of losing an arm or a leg.

John. And I would glory to surrender both to save my country! Have you ever heard The Incident of the French Camp?

Henry. No!

James. Give it to us, General.

John. I will, and may it stir some patriotism in your breasts. (*declaims*)

    You know we French stormed Ratisbon:
     A mile or so away,
    On a little mound Napoleon
     Stood on our storming day;

With neck out-thrust—you fancy how—
  Legs wide, arms locked behind,
As if to balance the prone brow,
  Oppressive with its mind.

Just as perhaps he mused, "My plans
  That soar, to earth may fall,
Let once my army-leader, Lannes,
  Waver at yonder wall,"—
Out 'twixt the battery smoke there flew
  A rider, bound on bound,
Full gallopping; nor bridle drew
  Until he reached the mound.

Then off there flung in careless joy,
  And held himself erect
By just his horse's mane, a boy;
  You hardly could suspect
(So tight he kept his lips compressed
  Scarce any blood came thro')—
You looked twice ere you saw his breast
  Was all but shot in two.

"Well," cried he, "Emperor! by God's grace
  We've got you Ratisbon!
The marshal's in the market-place,
  And you'll be there anon,
To see your flag-bird flap his vans
  Where I, to heart's desire,
Perched him!" The child's eye flashed; his plans
  Soared up again like fire!

The chief's eye flashed; but presently
  Softened itself, as sheathes
A film the mother eagle's eye
  When her bruised eaglet breathes:

"You're wounded!" "Nay," his soldier's pride
   Touched to the quick, he said:
"*I'm killed, sire!*" and his chief beside,
   Smiling, the boy fell dead!

Henry. Bravo!
James. I do feel more patriotic.
John. Was not that a glorious death? Let us give three cheers for the dear old flag of our country!
All. Hip! hip! hurrah!   (*Exeunt.*)

TRUE TO HIS COLORS.

[*For two boys,* JOHN *and* HENRY.]

John. How cold it is—ugh! How cold! And I haven't a cent to buy something to eat with. I am sure I don't see how mother and I are to get through the long winter. It is only December now; and three or four long dreary months must pass before we can look for anything like moderate weather again. Dear me! dear me! how I wish I could get money in some way or another! Now if I could only find some sort of employment, I'd be willing to work; but that is out of the question. I've tried and tried and tried; but it's all in vain. No one wants me, and no one cares for or believes a word of my story. I am too shabby to be respectable, they think; they have all provided for themselves. It's hard, hard, hard! Then I have a mother depending upon me. How can I see her suffer? To be sure I am offered a situation if I will denounce the stars and stripes, and deny my principles. But I shall not! Never! My dear mother would not allow me to do that. I would rather die first. Here in my breast have I carried this bright emblem of our country, (*shows flag*) and I shall never, never deny it. Woe unto those who would trail it in the dust! (*sees a purse on the ground*) Why, what is this? (*picks it up*) A purse, as I am alive! How fortunate! How lucky I was to see it! Surely kind Providence watches over me. How much

is there in it? Whew! A tremend—Ha! there comes some one.
I'll hide it. I'll—no; there's no one. It was but the wind.
Dear me! how frightened I am! My nerves are all of a tremble.
I quake and start at every noise. My head swims. Let me have
another look. What a great roll of bills! I'll count them.
Mother, dear mother, you are saved. Ah! One, two, three, four
five, six, seven, eight, nine, ten, eleven. Dear, dear, this is getting
exciting. Twelve, thirteen—oh, my!—fourteen, fifteen—fifteen
hundred dollars! What a fortune! Mother will be a grand lady
yet! Fifteen hundred dollars! But have I a right to keep it?
Is it mine? Ought I not to hunt out the real owner and return
him the money? Pshaw! what nonsense! Of course I ought
not. In spite of the temptation, I will stick to my colors and do
the right. Ah! there *is* some one, in good earnest. Where can
I hide the money? Dear me, I hope he won't notice me, I am so
confused!

Enter HENRY.

Henry (aside). Oh, dear! oh, dear! What shall I do? I am
afraid I shan't be able to find it at all. I have been to so many
places this morning that I really can't remember them all; and
nobody I have spoken with has seen it. Oh, dear! oh, dear!
What shall I do? Ah, here is some one; he may have seen it.
My good man, have you seen anything like a purse lying anywhere in the street? I have lost mine; and—and—No; I see
you haven't from your face. I——

John (aside). What shall I say? If I give it up I must lose all.
If I keep it mother and I need never want. Oh, what shall I say?
What shall I do? *(aloud)* N-no, sir; I—I—have *not* seen your
purse. *(aside)* Oh, why did I not tell the truth? I wish—But it
is too late now! Too late! *(aloud)* I am very sorry for you, I
assure you, sir; but I have not seen it.

Henry. Then I am lost! lost! It was my earnings on my last
cruise on board of a man-o'-war. Prize money and all. All was
earned in the service of Uncle Sam. Every cent I could get I
added to my little store; and it was with joy that I watched the
sum increasing day by day in hope that some time—But no, no!
it's all gone now—all gone now! Poor mother! poor mother!

John (*aside*). I can no longer conceal my deceit. I must tell him, let the consequences be what they may. Oh, sir, forgive me! I have deceived you. I have told you a falsehood! I *did* find the money; and God forgive me for not resisting the temptation sooner. I intended to keep it. I am a poor man, sir; it was a great temptation; but God be praised, I have conquered at last! I will be true to my colors! Here is your purse; take it! I have wronged you! Will you not forgive me?

Henry. What do I hear? My money? Thank God! thank God! Forgive you? Sir, you are a noble man! Forgive you? boy, heartily do I. It was indeed a great temptation, but you resisted it; and—But will you not let me know your name?

John. Do not ask me, I beseech you.

Henry. Surely you have no reason to be ashamed of it.

John. John Sedley is my name.

Henry. John Sedley! Surely my ears deceive me! John Sedley! Why, then you are my own cousin! I have been away fighting for the flag for four years. No wonder I didn't know you before.

John. Is it so indeed? Then once again I thank God for this temptation resisted; and I shall ever have faith in my motto: Stick to your colors through all temptations! (*Exeunt.*)

THE ARMY AND NAVY.

[*For two boys and a number of girls.*]

Enter a boy dressed in a soldier's uniform, bearing the American flag. If possible the Star-Spangled Banner or any other national air should precede his entrance.

Army. 'Tis mine to bear these stripes and stars
Amid our country's glorious wars!
'Tis mine to guard her sacred rights;
To bear her fame my heart delights.

What noble names have graced her cause!
With deeds that won the world's applause?
Go back with me and count again
The names inscribed on history's fane.
Brave Warren—hear his last reply:
" 'Tis sweet for native land to die!"
Then hearken to the words of Hale
(Beneath his glance the tyrants quail!)
" 'Tis my regret that I can give
But one life that this flag may live!"
Last, but not least, in glory won,
Behold the name of Washington!
Equal in war as well as peace,
His hallowed fame shall never cease.
His name inspires to noble deeds,
His lesson now each patriot heeds.
The army be my love and pride;
I'd fall this glorious flag beside!

Enter a boy dressed in sailor costume, bearing the flag, and preceded by a national air as before.

Navy. Beneath this flag of stars so true
I wander o'er the waters blue!
'Tis mine our commerce great to guard,
And o'er our shores keep watch and ward.
What noble names are here enshrined,
What deeds of glory here we find!
Columbia's march is o'er the sea,
Dear flag, our hopes we place in thee!
Within my ears I hear once more,
Amid the din of cannon's roar,
Brave Lawrence, as he bids his men
Go rally for the fight again!
I hear him speak with blood-stained lip,
"Fight on! Oh, don't give up the ship!"
Such words as these the heart inspire,
And re-illume proud Freedom's fire!

How many's dying gaze hath set
Upon thy folds, with no regret,
Save that their hands could strike no more
The blow that would thy life restore!
My heart and hand I give to thee,
Flag of the land and of the sea!

Army. First in the van the soldier stands,
    The sailor next, I own!

Navy. To go where'er this flag commands
    The sailor's first, alone!

Army. Who guards the people's sacred rights
    When battle's call is loud?

Navy. Who o'er the howling billow fights
    When rises battle's cloud?

Army. 'Tis I protect the homes of all
    From tyrants far and near.

Navy. You on the land, I on the sea—
    That from their grasp I clear.

Army. When drums awake, then sword in hand
    I march to join the fray,
Where come the bold insulting foe
    In battle's stern array!

Navy. When piped to action, who so brave
    As he, the sailor true?
He sweeps the bounding wave to save
    The red, the white, the blue!

Army. The army first, I hold it true!

Navy. No! no! the navy first!

Enter a girl dressed as the Goddess of Liberty.

Liberty.   Hold, boys in blue!
What means this cry of first or last?
I heard both, as this way I passed.
My sons are you, in word and deed,
Allow me, pray, to intercede,
And stop this quarrel here begun,
I hope you only meant in fun.

You both have equal been to me,
One on the land, one on the sea.
'Twas you that won my worthy cause,
'Twas you that first maintained my laws.
To you I owe my life and breath,
You rescued me from wreck and death.
When first I called upon you both,
Each flew to guard me, nothing loth.
The names you honor I place high
Beneath the dome of Freedom's sky!
My hands were weak, when first assailed,
To do my work ye never failed.
Thro' suffering and pain and woe,
Thro' summer's sun and winter's snow,
Ye overthrew the tyrants foul,
And gave the pangs of war release;
Bringing to me, from land and sea,
The heavenly olive branch of Peace;
Thro' you the silver stars here strewn,
Have, one by one, in numbers grown.
Behold the States, in proud array appear,
Each State is symboled by the bright stars here.
                    (*pointing to the flag.*)

Enter a number of girls, each representing a State in the Union. Each one may bear a small banner bearing the name of the State she represents. The girls march and countermarch, then form on each side of the platform. If possible some patriotic march should be played.

Army.   See what a proud array in Union bound!
Navy.   All, all with peace and golden plenty crowned!
Liberty.   Thirteen was all, when first your might was shown;
             Behold to what a number they have grown!

             Enter COLUMBIA.

Columbia. All here, my children, as I see,—
             I bid you welcome, sweet, sweet Liberty.
                    (LIBERTY *and* COLUMBIA *shake hands.*)

Without your smiles these States had never thrived,
See how they now are blest! how each has strived.
There's little Rhody by the great New York.
   My family is large!
Here now you see North, South, and East,
   And West,—all neath my charge.
Do you remember when I sought your aid
To help me in the strife that tyrants made?

Columbia. I do; and these I gave (*pointing to* ARMY *and* NAVY)
   to nobly fight,
And win for you the battle for the Right!
Forever may they stand, united still,
With earnest zeal to proudly do your will.
The one on land to guard the homes we love,
The one on sea, o'er billows wild to rove.
United still, oh, may they ever be,
To fight the battles of the brave and free!

All join in singing this stanza to the air of "Columbia, the Gem of the Ocean."

We pledge them our love and devotion,
   Our Army and Navy so grand;
The one is the pride of the ocean,
   The other the boast of the land.
May the service united ne'er sever,
   But always to their colors prove true,
The Army and Navy forever,—
   Three cheers for the Red, White and Blue!
Three cheers for the Red, White and Blue!
Three cheers for the Red, White and Blue!
The Army and Navy for ever,—
Three cheers for the Red, White and Blue!
                      (*Exeunt omnes.*)

SHALL OUR MOTHERS VOTE?

Characters.—JOHN READY, JAMES ROSE, TOM SLOWBOY, SAM SLY, FRANK WILSON, CHARLEY BOARDMAN, FRANK BLACK (*colored*), ISAAC PEARL, PERCY KIMBALL, NORVAL YOUNG, MIKE SHEA.

JOHN READY *enters, followed by* SLOWBOY.

Ready. Treasury entirely empty, you say, Slowboy?

Slowboy. Not a dollar, not the minutest particle of scrip, not even that very small specimen of hard money, a nickel.

Ready. Where has it gone? It was only a month ago we collected the annual assessment.

Slowboy. And it was only last week we had our great debate on "The Influence of Peace," in which our members became so much interested that four panes of glass were broken, the looking-glass smashed, one chair received a broken back, and another received a compound fracture of one of its legs. Of course all these little eccentricities of genius must be paid for; and the treasury is empty. If this is one of the influences of peace, we had better change the subject.

Ready. The members were a little emphatic on that occasion; but it was a glorious debate; and the question, " Resolved, that Peace is the foundation of prosperity," was carried before we broke up.

Slowboy. Yes; and 'twas the peace party broke up the furniture, and smashed the windows.

Ready. Ah, Slowboy, I fear you bear malice; for you, if I recollect aright, were one of the war party.

Slowboy. My voice is still for war.

Ready. We must find some way to fill the treasury. I fear the members will not stand taxation.

Slowboy. With the storied memories of their plucky forefathers before them in this centennial year, I should say not a cent. It must be raised by fines. The peace party have carried the day. Let us have peace.

Ready. I do not understand you.

Slowboy. My plan is very simple. We are constantly interrupted in debate. There's that Sam Sly, for instance. Heretofore you have tried to suppress the interruption with the remark, "The gentleman is out of order!" Whereupon the *gentleman* subsides until he feels like breaking out again. And they do break out often, especially Sam. Now, I propose to fine a member for each and every interruption five cents. Some of them will find it impossible to keep quiet, and our treasury will fill rapidly.

Ready. That's quite an idea, if it can only be made to work.

Slowboy. I think it can. And if we succeed Sam Sly will pay dear for this night's debate.

Ready. Sam Sly again. Slowboy, I fear you are malicious. Sly is one of our best debaters; and because you do not agree on all points——

Slowboy (*angrily*). We agree on no point. He's a saucy, conceited chap that's forever interrupting. I never attempted to declaim in school but what he was at my elbow with his insulting——

Sly (*who has entered, stands at* Slowboy's *elbow*). Charcoal!

Slowboy. Oh, confound you, here you are.

Sly. Yes, here I am, Slowboy, ready to be confounded, if not convinced, by your arguments against mother suffrage. Good evening, Mr. President. (*to* Ready.)

Ready. Good evening, Sam. Are the boys coming?

Sly. Yes, sir, close at hand. "All saddled, all bridled, all fit for the fight." (*they retire up.*)

Enter Isaac Pearl *and* Frank Wilson.

Isaac. Lew Bunker caught him out on the fly.

Frank. Ah! what did he say to that? (*they pass to the left and whisper.*)

Enter Percy Kimball *and* Charley Boardman.

Percy. Does your mother know you're out?

Charley. He said that, did he? (*they pass to left and whisper.*)

Enter NORVAL YOUNG *and* MIKE SHEA, *followed by* FRANK BLACK.

Norval (*speaking as they enter*). Well done, brave archer.

Mike. He was out on the fly.

Black. Out on de fly! Away wid yer nonsense. Dat are Bunker can't fly—ain't got de wings.

Ready (*takes chair, and raps on table*). The meeting will please come to order. (*all sit*) In the absence of our secretary, with the minutes, it will be necessary——

James Rose (*outside*). Hold on a minute. Here I am.

Enter ROSE.

Slowboy. Seems to me the secretary is behind time. He should be fined. (ROSE *drops the book and stoops to pick it up.*)

Sly. Don't you see he is picking up the minutes he has lost?

Slowboy. Puns should be fined.

Ready. Order, gentlemen. The first business in order is the reading of records of the last meeting.

Sly (*jumping up*). I move, Mr. President, the reading be dispensed with. (*sits.*)

Slowboy (*jumping up*). Mr. President, I hope the motion will not prevail. (*sits.*)

Sly (*rising*). Mr. President, the records of our regular were read at our last special, when we voted to adjourn immediately after the reading. I don't see any necessity of reading them again, unless the gentleman who objects was unable to understand them at the last meeting. (*sits.*)

Slowboy (*jumping up*). Mr. President, does Sam Sly mean——

Ready (*rapping*). The gentleman is out of order. The calling of names is unparliamentary. Is the motion to omit the reading seconded?

Frank. Second the motion.

Sly. Question!

Slowboy. Mr. President——

All (*except* SLOWBOY, *president, and secretary*). Question! question!

Black. Question afore de meetin' house.

Mike. Oh, hush your pate!

Ready. It is moved and seconded that the reading of the records be dispensed with. All those in favor will manifest it by the usual sign. (*all raise hands except* SLOWBOY) Contrary minded. (SLOWBOY's *hand up*) It is a vote.

Black (*to* MIKE). Dat are fellow's just like a mule.

Mike. Always kicking up.

Slowboy. Mr. President, in view of the many interruptions by which the more orderly have been made to suffer, and in consequence of the low state of our treasury, I move, sir, that during our deliberations and discussions this evening any member interrupting another during the progress of debate, shall be fined for each and every offence the sum of five cents. (*sits. All groan.*)

Sly (*rising*). Mr. President, although I seldom agree with the views of the gentleman, yet I am willing.

Several. Question! question!

Ready. The question is called for. Those in favor of the motion will manifest it. (*all hands up*) Carried. We will now proceed with the debate. (*reads*) "Resolved, that the good of mankind, the purity of the ballot-box, and the interest of society demand that our mothers shall vote." Mr. Isaac Pearl will open in the affirmative, Mr. Percy Kimball in the negative. (*sits.*)

Pearl. Mr. President, this is the age of progress, and I think the literary debaters of this society in the selection of the resolution on which I have the honor to speak in the affirmative here, have shown a commendable spirit of enterprise, which will be rewarded by the grateful plaudits of a ransomed nation, when woman, granted her rights, shall wield with man an equal power in the government of this enlightened community. (*cries of* "Good! good!")

Slowboy. Fines! fines! Mr. President, this is out of order. Put down Sly and——

Ready. Order!

Pearl. And who should have the first place in the march of reform? Who are best fitted to have a voice in the government? Who are heaven-born electors? Our mothers, sir. Is not their first duty government? Who have governed the greatest men that ever lived? Mothers. They teach our infant lips the language of our country. They lead our infant steps in the path of duty. Give them the ballot, and their influence will make better laws. Give them the ballot, and the ward-room and the election-boxes will be cleansed of corruption. Give them the ballot, and society will be an ever-changing spectacle of wrongs crushed out, and reforms working goodness, purity, and peace, while justice, exalted to the highest place, shall ever crown the earnest worker with the laurels of victory! (*cries of* "Good!" PEARL *sits*.)

Black (*to* MIKE). Dat's so. It jes takes de bullets to crush de spe'tacles, an—an——

Mike. Whist yer blarney. Ye's on the other side.

Ready. Mr. Percy Kimball has the floor.

Percy (*rising*). Mr. President and gentlemen, are we prepared to accept the views of the gentleman who has preceded me, and forever submit to petticoat government? He has spoken eloquently, I admit; but, sir, truth is above the rapid utterances of an impassioned harangue, which, I doubt not, has been compiled from all the speeches of the last fifty years. What are we to be forever tied to our mothers? are we to give up our coats and beavers? (*cries of* "Good!" *from speakers on negative side*.)

Sly (*rising*). Mr. President——

Slowboy (*jumping up*). An interruption! fine him. Mr. Secretary, put down Sam Sly five cents.

Sly. Mr. President, I rise to a point of order.

Ready. State your point, Mr. Sly.

Sly. The gentleman who has the floor has introduced such wild fashions—striff-crowned coats and long-tailed beavers—as to seriously affect the aspect of the question. I respectfully ask that he stick to the question.

Sly (*rising*). Mr. President, sir; I should be ungrateful to the mother that bore me did I not pronounce her worthy to stand forth, clothed with the right to raise her voice and cast her vote in the government of our glorious land. What has man accomplished for the good of mankind, the purity of the ballot-box, and the welfare of society, that women, and, foremost of all, our mothers, could not accomplish, but give them the opportunity? What have they not done already? Ask the millions of heroes who fought and bled for freedom where they caught their first inspiration. They will tell you at their mother's knee. Ask the free and enlightened voter who taught him to carefully probe political questions, and pluck the wheat from the chaff. He will tell you 'twas a wife's, a mother's, or a sister's influence. Can any work prosper without their aid? Is not society purified by their presence? Are they not in this movement gathering to their aid the eloquence and energy of the best and noblest of men? Be just! Be generous! Stand by the mothers who always stand by us; who guard and guide and teach us. We knew none better in our youth; we can choose none better when we reach the summit of a boy's ambition—the right to vote! (*sits. Applause.*)

Slowboy. I move we vote on the merits of the question.

Sly. Second the motion.

Ready. All in favor of adopting the resolution will manifest it in the usual manner. (*all but those who speak in the negative hold up hands*) Contrary minded. (*negative vote*) It is a vote.

Black. Say, Mike, was she guilty or not guilty?

Mike. Oh, whist your blarney.

Slowboy. Mr. President, I'd like to have the secretary read the list of fines.

Rose (*reads*). Mike Shea five cents; Tom Slowboy forty cents.

Slowboy. Just my luck.

Sly. Mr. President, I move we now adjourn.

Boardman. Second the motion.

Ready. Carried. (*Exeunt all.*)

THE OLD FLAG.

Characters.—JOHN, WILLIAM, *and* GEORGE.

Enter the three boys, all carrying flags.

William (*sing or speak*).

  Lift the flag, and join the song,
   One united nation;
  Union now, and evermore,
   Hear it all creation.

Wave the starry banner high;
Strike our colors, never,
Here we stand to live or die,
The stripes and stars forever.

John. Isn't it a beautiful flag, boys? We have a chart of the flags of all nations at home, but I think none can equal our dear star-spangled banner.

William. Always beautiful—always graceful. I wonder when it was first used?

George. It was ordered by Congress, June 14, 1777, "That the flag of the thirteen United States be thirteen stripes, alternate red and white; that the union be thirteen stars, white in a blue field, representing a new constellation;" but it was not used until the surrender of Burgoyne, in October of the same year.

John. Hurrah! Baptized in victory over the tyrant. What wonder wherever it waves freedom is triumphant?

William. Had we no flag before that, George?

George. Of course. Previous to the passage of the stamp act, the ordinary English ensign was used. The first distinct one I know anything about was in the year 1775. It bore the inscription, "George Rex, and the liberties of America."

John. Rather a contradiction, that.

George. You know that the colonies were not united at that time. The newspapers of the day were headed with a curious emblem, to show the necessity of union.

William. What was it? I never heard of it.

George. A rattlesnake, divided into thirteen parts, with the motto, "Join, or die." After the union of the colonies it was changed into a snake about to strike.

John. How curious

George. Paul Jones adopted the rattlesnake on a yellow field, with the motto, 'Don't tread on me," for a flag for his fleet. But, before he sailed, George Washington had assumed command of the young army of the colonies; and on the first of January, 1776, flung to the breeze, on Boston Heights, the flag known as the great Union.

William. Was that our glorious Stars and Stripes?

George. The stripes, but not the stars. In their place were the crosses of St. Andrew and St. George.

John. I should not have thought that Washington would have tolerated anything so British.

George. You must remember that we were then British subjects. After our fathers so gallantly threw off the yoke of the tyrant, those emblems were no longer appropriate, and the stars and stripes were adopted.

William. I wonder how, in those prosaic times, they ever came to do anything so romantic as to

> Stripe its pure celestial white
> With streakings of the morning light.

George. The flag used by the army was red, and that by the navy white; and I suppose they united the two.

John. Good! Union ever seemed to be their motto, even in comparatively little things.

William. Well, they could not have a better, for it has been gloriously proved that in "union there is strength."

John. Yes.

> United we stand, and divided we fall,
> Has made and preserved us a nation,

and has nearly quadrupled the galaxy of stars on the flag, which now I shall love more dearly than ever from having gained so much information about it.

William. By-the-bye, it was a good idea that of adding a star for every new State. I wonder they did not add a stripe too.

George. That *was* the *original* idea.

John. Why was it not carried out?

George. In 1794, after Vermont and Kentucky had been admitted into the Union, the flag was changed to fifteen stripes and fifteen stars, and remained so until 1818, although five or six new States had been added.

William. I suppose they did not anticipate the addition of so many stripes, and it would have made our flag too large?

George. Yes; but that was not the reason. They wished to recall the past, and recognize the original thirteen States which had gained our independence, and at the same time to show the progress which the infant republic had made since then.

John. And the result is our gallant banner. Who would not rally round such a flag? I feel as though I should like to give a hearty three times three for it.

William. How could any one dishonor it? It makes my blood boil to think of its ever having been trampled in the dust.

George. It is known and honored all over the world, from the north pole to the south—from the rising to the setting sun. And it is known, not as the flag of Massachusetts, New York or South Carolina, but as the *American* standard. It is an emblem, not of the growth of cotton or corn, or the development of iron, but of a gigantic strength—of unparalleled resources, of unexampled activity, of an undying progress, which knows neither North, South, East, or West, but where each is swallowed up in the great whole—the *one* nation of many States—the UNION.

William. How it must make one's heart swell to behold it, after having long been denied the sight.

John. I have heard some who were long prisoners of war away from home describe, in the most touching language, their feelings when they again beheld it.

George. Yes; it is no longer a mere piece of bunting, but it is fraught with sacred memories of all that they hold most dear, and is an earnest of friends, and home, and country.

William (waving his flag).

> Vainly the prophets of Baal had rended it,
> Vainly his worshippers prayed for its fall,
> Thousands have died for it, millions defended it,
> Emblem of justice and mercy to all.

But I pray that from this time forth forevermore, it may indeed be a symbol of unity, and that no more blood of martyrs may be needed to hallow its memory or defend its purity.

George With all my heart I echo the wish that never more shall national sins need to be washed out in national blood. I believe we are God's nation. Our free institutions proclaim it—our free religion proclaims it; but there are several remarkable coincidences. Did it never strike you that our old flag was significant of this?

John. How do you make that out?

George. The red, white and blue are typical colors we meet with all through the Bible. The *red*, the blood of the Lamb, slain for our ransom; the *white*, the garments of the glorified saints; the *blue*, the firmament which his hand has spread over us, to conceal the glories which await the final victor.

William. Or take them in their figurative sense. The *love* of God toward his people and the *purity* and *devotion* which he requires of them.

John. Bravo! Will. I'll have to help you out, too. My little brother asked mother, the other day, whether the big star in the middle of the union was not the same one that led the shepherds to where the baby Jesus lay; and whether all the little stars were not going there too.

George. That's not a bad idea. If we place Jesus in our midst for a leader, and gather round Him, the country will be safe enough.

William. Do not the *stripes* represent the chastisement which has been inflicted on us, wherewith we are healed; and the *stars* show the final brightness to which we shall attain?

John. You are coming rapidly on, Will.

William. I hope so, for I have made up my mind to endeavor, by serving this Captain with all my heart, to be ready to serve my country, should any peril threaten her, when manhood brings the proper strength.

George. Did all do so we would find that, even as God delivered Israel from the *Red* Sea, guided them by the *white* cloud, or Shekinah, through the dreary wilderness to the *blue* waters of the Jordan, so would he deliver us from all peril, guide the ship of state safely over the troubled waters of party politics, and bring her at last, tried and strengthened, to a place at the head of the nations.

John. I see now that without *purity* and *devotion* to God mere *love* to our country will not make us truly brave.

George. No; but we can unite these; and even as we are commanded to have "One Lord, one faith, one baptism," so may we have "One people, one constitution, and one flag."

William. Flag of the free heart's hope and home,
  By angel hands to valor given,
Thy stars have lit the welkin dome,
  And all thy hues were born in heaven!
Forever float that standard sheet
  Where breathes the foe that falls before us,
With Freedom's soil beneath our feet,
  And Freedom's banner streaming o'er us!

1776—1876.

[*For two girls.*]

[Try and dress *en costume* of the period. A full dress of the old Revolutionary period would be an oddity.]

Enter '76, advancing to the front of the stage. 1876 follows at a little distance, when '76, turning and catching sight of her, exclaims:

1776. Laws me! What horrible-looking creetur's this?

1876. Horrible looking, indeed! What a blessing some folks can't see themselves as others see them. Such a want of style! (*looking '76 all over*) such ignorance of fashion! and I do think our present modes are perfectly lovely! (*inspecting her own dress generally*) Why, you poor old fossil, what are you doing here?

1776. Doin'? why, lookin' round, to be sure; it runs in our blood to want to be lookin' round. Ever sence an old ancestor of mine took a twenty years' sleep, and waked up to find the whole airth turned topsy-turvy, some of us has come back every few years to find how things is goin' on. I'm mistress Rip Van Winkle, mum. (*jerking a low courtesy.*)

1876. Mrs. Rip Van Winkle! Ah! I didn't know such a troublesome habit ran in your family.

1776. Didn't know! Thank fortin' there's *somethin'* 1876 don't know. Here I've been wanderin' east, west, north, and south, lookin' on and sighin' over the times runnin' back'ard so, but never till now have I met man, woman, or child that owned up there was anythin' on this universe they didn't know. Young woman, I've hopes of you! But be you young?

1876. Young? Don't you perceive I am? What do you ask such a question as that for?

1776. 'Cause, between the *isn'ts* and the *ought-to-be's*, I'm all mixed up. I've followed gay-looking young creeturs, with their doll's bonnets on their top hairs, and a long curl hangin' over their shoulders, *pretty near* the same color as their hair, and I've thought, "Well, that gal's mother has taken a deal of pains to rig her out, sure! only it's a pity she's run off with her sister's gownd on, two or three yards too long;" when, lo and behold! she'd turn, and if her face wasn't forty or fifty, it ought to be! Laws! in *my* day children used to make believe they was growd folks, but growd folks didn't play they was children. We spun and wove, and kept the wolf from the door, and the Indians too, while our men fought for a free home. We didn't keep our hair in a box, and put it on arternoons, and try to pass off for sweet sixteen. So look er here, *be* you young?

1876. Dear me! how excruciating to one's auricular organs to hear such ungrammatical language! Don't you know it is not proper to say "*be* you"?

1776. Yes, there you go ag'in. Sich talkin'! Why, half the time I don't know what new-fangled tongue people's got. Somebody says to me, "When did you arrive?" I didn't *arrive* at all; I come. Why couldn't they ask me straight? "How is your marm?" I said. "Well, she's convalescing." "Conva—what? dear me! is it ketchin'?" says I. Do you think, the woman was just a-gittin' well, and that child didn't know how to tell it. "Where's your dad?" says I to the 'pot'cary's boy. "He's engaged in a consultation, ma'am." Land alive! didn't I pity the poor creetur that had to have that done to him? And after all he just meant his father was a-talkin' with another man.

1876. You seem to be entirely oblivious to the extraordinary progress of the age. Philology has become a popular science, and language improves proportionately.

1776. Dear suz! don't it kinder make your mouth ache to say all that? I don't calkerlate on understandin' it, no mor'n I do that thing the lightnin' travels on.

1876. The telegraph I presume you refer to.

1776. The tell-a-lie'd be nearer it. Maybe I'll give in you've got some new things; but no airthly power'll ever make me believe a body at one end of a string can hear what's said at t'other, three miles off.

1876. I don't think you understand the principle.

1776. No, there can't be no principle to people who go on so. Why, when I was a gal, I had my picter painted—took a man three weeks, and used a power of paint; and here to-day some onprincipled feller told me to set down, and he'd do my likeness in five minutes, and never do a livin' thing himself but walk round the room with a watch in his hand.

1876. Did you comply with his request?

1776. Comply! I guess I didn't! I jest sot right down and waited till he'd fixed up a little brass cannon and p'inted it at me, and then I left. I said I'd be shot if I staid.

1876. Excuse me, but we call such expressions as that "slang."

1776. Slang! I didn't say "slang," I said "shot," and meant it, too. I allers say what I mean. I never put on no airs. Some of the girls in my time—you know there's fools in every age—when they was goin' out to tea, used to think 'twas pretty to lisp; so they'd keep sayin', "thsoft thsoap, thsoft thsoap," to get their tongues right; but I didn't. I never soft soaped nobody, to my knowin'.

1876. Then you couldn't have taken much interest in the political partisans of the day, or you'd found abundant need of saponaceous literature.

1776. My! that's poetry, isn't it? I can't say I ever took to that much. I tried once to make a verse, and the first line ended with pilgrim. I tried four weeks to find a rhyme, and couldn't think of anything but Uncle Jim, and I didn't want him in, so I had to give it up.

1876. Women were not so universally blue stockings then as now?

1776. Well, no; we wore gray mostly—sometimes white, Sundays.

1876. I mean, women did not write as they do nowadays.

1776 Well, I dunno; there's a difference in hands. Mostly they could write their names pretty fair.

1876. Dear me! there's no such thing as making such an antediluvian petrifaction understand. I mean, women did not compose books and have them published as they do now.

1776. Laws! I guess they'd been put in the pillory for anything half so disgraceful. Why, our minister writ a book. 'Twas the greatest thing! You couldn't sense a bit of it; and I guess no woman'd 'a' dared say she was equal to that in them days.

1876. Man's fancied superiority, I am happy to say, is giving way before woman's assertion of equal rights.

1776. Equal rights! Why, I believe in that. I believe a woman has just as much right to be a woman as a man has to be a man. I believe a woman has just as much right to mind her Bible and obey her husband as he has to mind his and honor her. I don't see what more you want.

1876. More! Pretty equal rights that would be! But with your old-fashioned notions you cannot be expected to understand the strides of an age that has progress written on its banners, and claims for women just the same privileges it does for men.

1776. Oh, that's what it means, is it? I saw an old flag as I came along with "Woman's Rights" and "Woman's Votes" on it, but I thought 'twas some new kind of riggin' they had to sell. I didn't s'pose it meant womenkind votin'.

1876. Well, it did mean just that. If a woman hasn't as good a right to vote as a man, I'd like to know the reason.

1776. Should you, dear? I'm sorry I can't tell you; but this 'ere progress is gittin' too much for my head altogether. I dunno any reason, 'cept it'll take an awful time to git through votin' when that day comes.

1876. I don't know why it should.

1776. Why, you see, things'll git to that pitch a woman'll want her say first—'twouldn't be havin' her rights if she didn't—so *he*'ll have to stay home and 'tend the babies while *she* goes to the polls. Then she'll jest run into the neighbor's for a minit—that's half a day, you know; and when his turn comes he'll get to argufyin' on the nashunal debt, and that'll take up t'other half. And there'll be Bridget goin' on like old Ireland 'cause she's got to wait till next day for her chance. Why, there's no calkerlatin' when they'll get through, that fashion.

1876. No need worrying about that. Of course there'll be some improved method of casting votes devised when the ladies take hold of it.

1776. I s'pose so. Some patent fixin' like enough, runnin' round pickin' up votes by steam. It won't have my breath to take away, though.

1876. No, you belong to a slow age. How glad I am I didn't live in '76.

1776. Bless you, dear! I hope you'll enjoy your rights. But what a mercy I wasn't born in 18—. (*Exeunt.*)

THE CHIEF'S RESOLVE.

Characters.—CARABASSET, *an Indian;* FATHER RASLES (*pronounced Rawl.*)

Carabasset (*alone*).

The night is on the wane, and man now sinks
Into forgetfulness. It is the hour
When e'en the pale-face ceases to molest,
And, like the dreaded catamount when gorged,
Doth slumber heavily. A fitting time
To blot out with their blood all memory
Of wrong—if to blot out were possible.
How many now lie down to dream of prey
That never can be theirs—of valued furs—
And of the scalps of red men, the reward
Of perfidy, to be exchanged for gold!
Soon must ye pass into a dreamless sleep!
Yes, it is time we raised the tomahawk
In defence of this our native land!

Enter RASLES.

Rasles (aside).

Ill-fated warrior, doomed, alas! too soon
To drain that bitter cup which all must drain,
When the companion, nearest and most loved,
Lives but in memory. I'll speak to thee. (*to* CARABASSET)
My Carabasset! one, whose feeble hand
Was once retained by thine in friendly pressure,
Comes to assuage thy sorrows. Son, look up,
And ease this troubled heart.

Carabasset.

Away, and leave me!
Who mourns for Carabasset? Is he not
Like the scathed pine on which the flame hath fed
Till it is sapless, naked, and decaying?

Rasles.

Oh, say not thus! for it shall bloom again,
Nourished with the dew from heaven. Come, behold me!

Carabasset.

Ha! of the pale-faced race! I hate ye all.
What, art thou tired of life, to venture thus
Beneath my deadly grasp?

Rasles.

Strike, if thou canst!
My son, my son, hast thou forgotten Rasles?
He on whose knees it was thy joy to climb
In thy young days?—who gave thee Rena, too?

Carabasset.

Rena!—and was it thou?—yes—I remember—
One was the friend of red men; one—and *but* one.
Old man, I will not harm thee—go in peace.

Rasles.

And leave thee here in wretchedness! I cannot.
Come, be thyself again, nor waste the hours

In brooding o'er thy wrongs. It is in love
That the Great Spirit chastens. Come, return.

Carabasset.

Return! who now will welcome Carabasset?
Where is the hand that bathed his aching temples,
And spread fresh rushes for his weary limbs?
Where is the eye that lighted at his coming?
Where is the form that welcomed his embrace?
What monsters are ye all to leave me thus!

Rasles.

Again, let me entreat thee to return.
Let not the bravest of the Norridgewocks,
He who for fortitude hath been so famed,
Give way to this excess. Thy warriors wait
Impatient to behold thee. Ah, the sound
That comes upon the breeze denotes too well
How high they prize the noble Carabasset.
Would it were less; for now, inflamed with rage,
They all would madly rush where you direct.

Carabasset.

Ha! is it thus? Then they are truly brothers.

Rasles.

Forbear, my son; give up thy cruel purpose.
Let not the act of one abandoned wretch
Bring ruin on the innocent. Forbear.
We will demand the assassin; rest assured
They will not dare refuse to give him up.
Thus justice can be satisfied, and still
The cradle's sleep be quiet as before.

Carabasset.

As well go ask the fierce and ravenous bear
To yield her young: they'll mock at your petition.
They hold their blood too precious to be shed
For that which flows within a red man's veins.
No—all shall perish!

Rasles.

    Hear me, Carabasset!
Hear me—if not in pity to the whites,
In pity to your race. Your foes are mighty.
They will not idly sit, and bare their heads
To the uplifted tomahawk. Their bands,
Well armed and numerous, will seize each pass,
And hem ye in. Courage availeth not
Against a host; and, when your warriors fall,
Their wives, their children, all that they hold dear,
Must perish with them.

Carabasset.

    Well, then, be it so.
Better to perish thus than breathe as slaves.
Talk not of mercy—they have shown us none;
And should we spare them, they would call it fear.
Yet often have I spared them. Who can say
That Carabasset slew except in battle?
Oft through the snow, for many a weary day,
The trembling, helpless captive have I borne
Back to its mother's arms, nor asked for ransom.
Oft struck aside the tomahawk's keen edge,
That the red warrior brandished o'er their young;
Ay, plunged into their dwellings, wrapped in flames,
And drew them forth to life and liberty.
And yet for this what hath been the return?

Rasles.

Son, thou hast acted nobly—act so still;
Forgive e'en this, and——

Carabasset

    Hast thou ever loved?
And was the loved one torn from thy embrace?

Rasles.

Oh, spare me, spare me! Thou hast touched a chord
That now for years hath slumbered. (*turns from him with
 emotion.*)

Carabasset.

       Ha! thou hast.
I too have loved, and those I loved were murdered.
The voice that pleads for others failed to move
Their flinty hearts—the child, too—none were spared;
And yet the coward lives who gave the blow!
My warriors call me!

    Rasles.

    Where shall we meet again?

    Carabasset.

Where meet the brave! for there the red man rests,
When he hath sung his death-song, and gone down
To the dark valley. There we shall renew
Our song of joy and triumph; there rejoin
Our brothers, who have perished in the battle.
Yes, there we'll meet again! for who would live,
When all he loved were torn from his embrace
And he was deemed so vile, that 'twas denied him
Even to guard the sod that wrapped their bones! (*he goes out.*)

    Rasles.

Gone! deaf to my entreaties; then 'tis over!
Would that a single victim might suffice!
Though few the drops that creep within these veins,
They should flow freely, could they flow for all. (*Exit.*)

THE VETERAN.

[*For two boys,* CAPTAIN HARDY *and* NATHAN.]

Nathan. Good morning, Captain. How do you stand this hot weather?

Captain. Lord bless you, boy, it's a cold-bath to what we had at Monmouth. Did I ever tell you about that air battle?

Nathan. I have always understood that it was dreadful hot that day?

Captain. Lord bless you, boy, it makes my crutch sweat to think on't—and, if I didn't hate long stories, I'd tell you things about that air battle sich as you wouldn't believe, you rogue, if I didn't tell you. It beats all natur how hot it was.

Nathan. I wonder you did not all die of heat and fatigue.

Captain. Why, so we should if the reg'lars had only died first; but, you see, they never like the Jarseys, and wouldn't lay their bones there. Now, if I didn't hate long stories, I'd tell you all about that air business, for you see they don't do things so nowadays.

Nathan. How so? Do not people die as they used to?

Captain. Lord bless you, no. It beat all natur to see how long the reg'lars would kick after we killed them.

Nathan. What! kick after they were killed? That does beat all natur, as you say.

Captain. Come, boy, no splitting hairs with an old continental; for, you see, if I didn't hate long stories, I'd tell you things about this ere battle that you'd never believe. Why, Lord bless you, when Gineral Washington telled us we might gin it to 'em, we gin it to 'em, I tell you.

Nathan. You gave what to them?

Captain. Cold lead, you rogue. Why, bless you, we fired twice to their once, you see; and, if I didn't hate long stories, I'd tell you how we did it. You must know the reg'lars wore their close-bodied red coats, because they thought we were afeard on 'em; but we didn't wear any coats, you see, because we hadn't any.

Nathan. How happened you to be without coats?

Captain. Why, Lord bless you, they would wear out, and the States couldn't buy us any more, you see, and so we marched the lighter and worked the freer for it. Now, if I did not hate long stories, I could tell you what the Gineral said to me next day, when I had a touch of the rheumatiz from lying on the field without a blanket all night. You must know it was raining hard just then, and we were pushing on like all natur arter the reg'lars.

Nathan. What did the General say to you?

Captain. Not a syllable says he, but off comes his coat, and he throws it over my shoulders. "There, Captain," says he, "wear that, for we can't spare you yet." Now don't that beat all natur, hey?

Nathan. So you wore the General's coat, did you?

Captain. Lord bless your simple heart, no. I didn't feel sick arter that, I tell you. "No, Gineral," says I, "they can spare me better than they can you jest now; and so I'll take the will for the deed," says I.

Nathan. You will never forget this kindness, Captain.

Captain. Not I, boy! I never feel a twinge of the rheumatiz, but what I say, God bless the Gineral. Now, you see, I hate long stories, or I'd tell you how I gin it to a reg'lar that tried to shoot the Gineral at Monmouth. You know we were at close quarters, and the Gineral was right between the two fires.

Nathan. I wonder he was not shot.

Captain. Lord bless your ignorant soul, nobody could kill the Gineral; but, you see, a sneaking reg'lar didn't know this, and so he levelled his musket at him; and, you see, I seed what he was arter, and I gin the Gineral's horse a slap on the haunches, and it beats all natur how he sprung, and the Gineral all the while as straight as a gun-barrel.

Nathan. And so you saved the General's life.

Captain. Didn't I tell you nobody could kill the Gineral; but, you see, his horse was in the rake of my gun, and I wanted to get the start of that cowardly reg'lar.

Nathan. Did you hit him?

Captain. Lord bless your simple soul, does the thunder hit where it strikes? though the fellow made me blink a little, for he carried away part of this ear. See there! (*showing his ear*) now don't that beat all natur?

Nathan. I think it does. But tell me how is it that you took all these things so calmly. What made you so contented under your deprivations and hardships?

Captain. O, bless your young soul, we got used to it. Besides, you see, the Gineral never flinched nor grumbled.

Nathan. Yes, but you served without being paid.

Captain. So did the Gineral; and the States, you know, were poor as all natur.

Nathan. But you had families to support.

Captain. Aye, aye ; but the Gineral always told us that God and our country would take care of them, you see. Now, if I didn't hate long stories, I'd tell you how it turned out jest as he said, for he beat all natur for guessing right.

Nathan. Then you feel happy and satisfied with wat you have done for your country, and what she has done for you ?

Captain. Why, Lord bless you, if I hadn't left one of my legs at Yorktown, I wouldn't have touched a stiver of the States' money ; and, as it is, I am so old that I shall not need it long. You must know, I long to see the Gineral again ; for, if he don't hate long stories as bad as I do, I shall tell him all about America, you see ; for it beats all natur how things have changed since he left us.

THE SPIRIT OF '76

[*For two boys,* HARRY *and* ISRAEL ; *one represents an old soldier.*]

Harry (*brings a chair and seats himself by side of* ISRAEL). Good-morning, grandfather. In your regimentals, I see.

Israel. Ah ! Harry, my boy, ever anxious for the old man's comfort. Good boy ! (*patting his head*) Yes, I am in my regimentals, in my armor, Harry—in my armor. Do you know what day this is ?

Harry. Yes, grandfather ; your birthday. There is no danger of my forgetting that,—the 19th of April, your 95th birthday. Why, you are getting to be quite a man.

Israel. Ha ! ha ! ha ! yes, Harry, I am growing,—Harry, I'm growing. My mother was wont to say she should never be able to raise me. Poor mother ! what would she say to see me now ?

Harry. She would say what we all do ; that there's many a younger in years, older in feeling and appearance, than you.

Israel. Yes, Harry, this is my birthday ; but *that* is not why I wear my uniform. This is a birthday more memorable than mine,

—April 19th, 1775. You remember Lexington, Harry, where the first Yankee blood was shed for freedom?

Harry. Ay, that I do, grandfather!

Israel. My father was there, Harry, and at Bunker Hill too, beside the brave Warren. *That* is why I wear the uniform. But there is a sadder remembrance this day brings. It recalls the time when I first knew what it was to be an orphan. It was three years after the battle of Lexington, at Valley Forge. My mother died two years before, and through camp and battle I had followed my father, often without food for days; our uncovered feet leaving streaks of blood along the snow as we marched to winter quarters at Valley Forge. That dreadful winter of privation and suffering, boy! in all my life, I have never witnessed its equal. My father lay dying before the smouldering embers of the scanty watch-fire. His comrades were gathered about him, for he was a favorite with them all; but disease had overtaken him, and he was dying. He called me to him, placed his hand upon my head, blessed me, bade me be true to my country and my God, and without a struggle died. I threw myself upon the body of my only friend, deaf to all the kindly consoling words of my father's comrades,—those noble veterans,—when a commanding voice caused me to raise my head. There, with the last faint light of the dying fire playing on his face, stood Washington. Shall I ever forget that scene? I have followed to the grave the wife of my early manhood; I have stood beside the dying-bed of your mother, my darling daughter; but through all the long years of battle, of peace, of mourning, and of joy, I see our noble leader as he stood with uncovered head beside the body of my dead father. He spoke kind words to me, and bade me follow to his tent. I watched beside my dead until the frozen earth opened to receive it, then made my way to the tent of the General. As I drew near it, I heard his voice raised in prayer. Softly approaching, I looked in. There on his knees, with upraised hands, was Washington, pouring out his soul to Heaven. Harry, I never realized until then what all this fighting was for. I was but a boy then; but that scene struck the fire in my soul that has never slumbered. Harry, I remember your reading to me, but a few days ago, the raising of " Old Glory " in Fort Sumter by the brave Major Anderson; of his kneeling, and asking the protection of Heaven for that flag. And I thought then, that our country could have no braver defender in the hour of danger than that prayerful man.

Harry. Yes, grandfather; Anderson is indeed noble, daring, and faithful. But Valley Forge was but the beginning of your experience?

Israel. Yes, Harry; when we left Valley Forge I, for the first time, shouldered a musket. I was near the General when he met Lee returning from Monmouth; 'twas there I struck the first blow for liberty. When the General checked the retreat, and bade Lee return, we knew there was to be warm work. How our hearts leapt! And on we went; Washington leading, with his sword gleaming in the air, as we rushed upon the foe. Rank after rank met us, and down they went. No retreat then. (*staggering to his feet*) No retreat when a Yankee bayonet is fixed and a Yankee heart beats warm in the cause of liberty. (*sets back into chair.*)

Harry. Ah, grandfather, those were patriots in heart and deed; would we had as true now in this hour of our country's peril!

Israel. As true now? We have as true and warm patriots now as then. Let but a hand be raised against that flag, and young and old will spring from every section of our country to protect it. The spirit of '76 is not dead, and can never die in the hearts of a free people.

WILLIAM TELL.

[*For two males and one female.*]

Tell.   Ye crags and peaks, I'm with you once again.
I hold to you the hands you first beheld,
To show they still are free. Methinks I hear
A spirit in your echoes answer me,
And bid your tenant welcome to his home
Again. O sacred forms, how proud you look!
How high you lift your heads into the sky!

How huge you are! how mighty, and how free!
Ye are the things that tower, that shine; whose smile
Makes glad; whose frown is terrible; whose forms,
Robed or unrobed, do all the impress wear
Of awe divine. Ye guards of liberty,
I'm with you once again. I call to you
With all my voice. I hold my hands to you,
To show they still are free. I rush to you
As though I could embrace you.

ERNI *enters.*

Erni.   You're sure to keep the time
That comes before the hour.

Tell.   The hour
Will soon be here. O, when will Liberty
Be here, my Erni? That's my thought, which still
I find beside. Scaling yonder peak,
I saw an eagle wheeling near its brow
O'er the abyss; his broad-expanded wings
Lay calm and motionless upon the air,
As if he floated there without their aid,
By the sole act of his unlorded will,
That buoyed him proudly up. Instinctively
I bent my bow; yet kept he rounding still
His airy circle, as in the delight
Of measuring the ample range beneath
And round about; absorbed, he heeded not
The death that threatened him. I could not shoot!
'Twas liberty! I turned my bow aside,
And let him soar away.

Enter EMMA.

Emma. O, the fresh morning! Heaven's kind messenger,
That never empty-handed comes to those
Who know to use its gifts. Praise be to Him
Who loads it still, and bid it constant run
The errand of his bounty! Praise be to Him!

	We need his care, that on the mountain's cliff
	Lodge by the storm, and cannot lift our eyes,
	But piles on piles of everlasting snows,
	O'erhanging us, remind us of His mercy.

Tell. Why should I, Emma, make thy heart acquainted
With ills I could shut out from it ?—rude guests
For such a home! Here only we have had
Two hearts; in all things else—in love, in faith,
In hope, in joy, that never had but one!
But, henceforth, we must have but one here also.

Emma. O, William, you have wronged me—kindly wronged me.
Whenever yet was happiness the test
Of love in man or woman ? Who'd not hold
To that which must advantage him ? Who'd not
Keep promise to a feast, or mind his pledge
To share a rich man's purse ? There's not a churl,
However base, but might be thus approved
Of most unswerving constancy. But that
Which loosens churls ties friends, or changes them,
Only to stick the faster. William! William!
That man knew never yet the love of woman,
Who never had an ill to share with her.

Tell. Not even to know that would I in so
Ungentle partnership engage thee, Emma,
So *will* could help it; but necessity,
The master yet of will, how strong soe'er,
Commands me. When I wedded thee
The land was free! With what pride I used
To walk these hills, and look up to my God,
And bless Him that it was so! It was free—
From end to end, from cliff to lake, 'twas free!
Free as our torrents are that leap our rocks,
And plough our valleys, without asking leave;
Or as our peaks, that wear their caps of snow
In very presence of the regal sun.
How happy was it then! I loved

Its very storms. Yes, Emma, I have sat
In my boat at night, when, midway o'er the lake,
The stars went out, and down the mountain gorge
The wind came roaring. I have sat and eyed
The thunder breaking from his cloud, and smiled
To see him shake his lightnings o'er my head,
And think I had no master save his own.
You know the jutting cliff round which a track
Up hither winds, whose base is but the brow
To such another one, with scanty room
For two abreast to pass? O'ertaken there
By the mountain blast, I've laid me flat along,
And, while gust followed gust more furiously,
As if to sweep me o'er that horrid brink,
I have thought of other lands, whose storms
Are summer flaws to those of mine, and just
Have wished me there—the thought that mine was free
Has checked that wish, and I have raised my head,
And cried in thraldom to that furious wind,
"Blow on! This is the land of liberty!"

Emma. I almost see thee on that fearful pass,
And yet, so seeing thee, I have a feeling
Forbids me wonder that thou didst so.

Tell.   'Tis
A feeling must not breathe where Gesler breathes,
But may within these arms. List, Emma, list!
A league is made to pull the tyrant down,
E'en from his seat upon the rock of Altorf.
Four hearts have staked their blood upon the cast,
And mine is one of them.

THE VISIONS OF FREEDOM.

Characters.—GLORIA, *Goddess of Freedom;* RUBINA, *her Counsellor of War;* SERENA, *her Counsellor of Peace;* QUEEN MAB *of Dreamland;* DROWSA, OBLIVIA, SOMNA, SOOTHA, *Dream Spirits;* ART, INDUSTRY, MUSIC, PLENTY, SERENA's *Attendants;* REVENGE, DISCORD, CRUELTY, *and* HATRED, RUBINA's *Attendants. Action supposed to have occurred in Dreamland. Green bank,* C. *Behind this a small platform about six inches high.* SCHOLARS *seated* R. *and* L. *of stage.*

Scholars (repeat in concert).
Slumber o'er earth is sending
  Its realm of sweet repose;
The stream of life, rest-tending,
  In peace through Dreamland flows;
Where waiting and caressing,
With varied visions blessing,
Dream Spirits vigils keep;
Dream Spirits vigils keep;
Their vigils keep, their vigils keep.

Enter, R., DROWSA *and* OBLIVIA; L., SOMNA *and* SOOTHA; *then,* R., QUEEN MAB, *who stands* C.

Queen Mab. Spirits of Dreamland, once again we meet,
  Our round of nightly revel to repeat.
  O'er earth when locked in sleep's warm, close embrace;
  Since time began the genius of our race
  Has had the power fearlessly to sway
  The visionary sceptre all obey.
  The mighty monarch, who, with tyrant frown,
  Upholds the burden of his weighty crown;
  The fierce-browed warrior who relentless slays,
  And, bathed in blood, his vows to Moloch pays;

Haughty and lowly, powerful and weak,
Under mysterious spells our guidance seek.
Sweet sister spirits, Dreamland opens wide,
Yet Justice guards it well on every side ;
Over the pure we rosy visions throw,
Around the base a sea of troubles flow.
Ere forth you glide to ply your happy arts,
Your Queen would learn the secrets of your hearts;
Who hie to sport, with mischievous intent,
And who on graver ministries are bent.

Sootha. I've an old miser under watchful care,
With sordid soul, of generous impulse bare,
Who nightly feasts, with avaricious eyes,
Where treasured gold in rare profusion lies ;
Who revels o'er his fast-increasing store,
Chuckles with glee, yet wistful sighs for more.
Starvation's image in a den so bare,
It seems a fit abode for dark despair.
Into his sleep I glide, disturb his rest,
Rattle his treasure, till with fear possest,
As frightful visions thick and thicker press,
He trembling wakes his idol to caress.

Oblivia. Fair Queen, a toiling student I enchain,
And with my art refresh his weary brain ;
Up Wisdom's heights I lead him by the hand,
And show him visions of the promised land ;
Fair fields of learning spread before his gaze ;
For him the realm of science set ablaze ;
Ope Fame's grand temple, Honor's scroll unroll,
And tell the triumphs of the trusting soul,
Till hope reanimates the wasting fire
With earnest zeal and conquering desire.

Somna. I guard a trusting maiden, young and fair,
Whom Love has tangled in his silken snare ;
Spread rosy dreams amid her sleeping hours,
And lead her captive through a land of flowers ;

Adorn her hero with true manly pride,
And of the future ope the portal wide,
While smiles of pleasure o'er her sweet face creep,
And blissful words betray her secret deep.
With rare delight her day-dreams I repeat,
And make her young life's round of love complete.

Drowsa. Oh, I've a task, fair Queen, will love secure.
Last night I visited, with visions pure,
A weary mother, who, for many a day,
Watched o'er the cradle where her dear babe lay,
Wasting with fever, till the unseen Hand
Took it in kindness to a better land.
Long has she mourned its loss, with wakeful eyes,
Fast-falling tears, low, sad, and bitter cries.
Last night she slept, and then, in vision's charms,
I crept, and laid her babe within her arms.
Content she rested, with a smile so sweet,
I go to-night this comfort to repeat.

Queen Mab. Your zeal, industrious spirits, we applaud;
Your chosen missions meet with full accord;
Yet for this night we have a task so grand,
Your Queen would all your energies command.

Somna. We wait your pleasure.
Oblivia.   All our arts employ.
Drowsa. Set us what tasks you will.
Sootha.   We'll serve with joy.

Queen Mab. Thanks, sisters! To our confidence draw near,
And list our secret with attentive ear.
Freedom's fair Goddess, Gloria, in doubt,
Her fair Republic, restless, roams about,
Seeking a talisman to life prolong,
And make her youthful charge wax brave and strong.
Close at her side Rubina—crafty maid—
Whose fire-lit eyes gloat over War's dread trade,
Plies her bold speech, unchecked by fear of frown,
Counselling deeds of conquest and renown;

While calm Serena, long to Peace allied,
Whose gentle influence stretches far and wide,
Recounts the glories of a land at rest,
With sterling Industry's rich harvests blest.
Wavering betwixt the gentle and the bold,
By turns rebellious, and by turns controlled,
Poor Gloria wanders long, in dire distress,
Which counsellor to choose her realm to bless.
Old Custom gives to us prophetic power,
To guide by vision in the trying hour.
And so to-night, o'er Gloria's doubting heart,
Fair sister spirits, we will ply our art,
Lure her to Dreamland, and in phantom light
Illume her path, and guide her to the right.
Stand close! she comes! the light winds bear along
The martial burden of her triumph song.
(*retire, and form behind bank.*)

Scholars (*in concert*).
Blest is the land where Freedom rears,
 'Neath heaven's blue arching dome
For Labor's sons of every clime,
 Her proud and happy home!
Beyond the reach of tyrant rule,
 Free are the hands we raise!
Onward we move, with joyous song
 Of thankfulness and praise.
 Blest is the land, etc.

Enter, L., GLORIA, *attended by* RUBINA *and* SERENA, *followed by Attendants.*

c. GLORIA.

R. RUBINA.   SERENA. L.

Attendants.
* * * *

* * * *
Attendants.

Gloria. Yes, mine, all mine, this bounteous land,
    So rich in varied blessings that command
    Homage from all. The mighty of the earth
    Must stoop to thee, O land of lowly birth!
    Thy mountains rise in majesty and pride;
    In royal state thy valleys open wide;
    Thy broad, expansive waters, spreading free,
    Embrace the bosom of the mother sea.
    Out of a fruitful earth thy harvests rise;
    Out leaps the golden ore with glad surprise!
    Over thy broad domains, with ceaseless hum,
    Labor's grand armies ever conquering come,
    While rare Invention opes its secret heart,
    And Genius rears its monumental art!
    O, land of promise! Gloria's inmost prayer
    Could ask no more than thy fair fate to share.
    Sweet counsellors, let Wisdom quick contrive
    Some plan this happy state to keep alive.

Rubina. A nation's life, fair mistress, action craves;
    Cold, sluggish apathy the blood enslaves.
    Renown's the rock on which to rear a state.
    Rubina's counsel is for conquest straight.

Gloria. Conquest, Rubina! Thine's a sorry jest.
    We have no quarrels; friends with all we rest.

Rubina. Ay; but to win renown, with fair excuse,
    Strike at the shadow of some old abuse
    Among our neighbors; or, with slight parade
    Of justice, boldly on their borders raid.
    Quick to revenge, their warlike hearts upspring—
    "To arms! to arms!" they cry. Their weapons ring;
    On us they march, a fast-increasing band,
    Till in the confines of our realm they stand.
    "Quick! to repel invasion!" then our cry;
    Alarming signals flash out fierce and high.
    From east and west, from north and south, outpour
    The sons of Freedom, in their strength secure,

    Drive back the foe; in turn invade their fold;
    Until their fate victoriously we hold.

Gloria. And then—

Rubina.   And then, boldly for ransom claim
    A portion of their realm in Freedom's name.

Gloria. What says Serena?

Serena.   'Tis a crafty plot,
    And full of wickedness. I like it not.
    Freedom's a name too sacred to enfold
    A hungering appetite for greed and gold.
    What conquest gains is ne'er enriched by toil;
    Ensanguined earth is but a sterile soil.
    Rubina's counsel, and her bold device,
    Would purchase glory at a bloody price.

Rubina. Serena, pause! thou hast no right to frown,
    With thy cold-hearted words, my counsel down.
    No crafty plot I weave to bring disgrace,
    But loftly plans to glorify the race.
    Let War once set his standard in the field,
    With strength and valor blazoned on his shield,
    The roar of cannon and the clash of steel,
    Shall glad the nation with triumphant peal,
    And strong and mighty conquerors enroll
    Heroic deeds on her historic scroll.

Serena. While o'er the land the blood of her dear sons—
    Conquest's sad recompense—in horror runs.
    Forbear, Rubina. Gracious mistress, Might
    Should ever wield its strong arm for the Right.
    Let not Rubina's counsel carry weight,
    Lest angry discord rend your lofty state.

Rubina. Insult again——

Gloria.   Nay, nay, Rubina. Pause;
    Thou hast had ample time to urge thy cause.
    With patience curb a while thy fiery mood;
    We'll ponder well thy influence for good.

Speak thou, Serena. Canst thou find release
For our perplexity in ways of peace?

Serena. Ay, Peace, fair mistress, is the fount of health,
Whence flow the streams of happiness and wealth
That bless a nation. In its waters fair,
Drowned are the pangs of life-corroding care;
Cheered and refreshed is Duty's faithful heart,
In Labor's trials strong to take its part.
O, happy Gloria! o'er this blest domain,
With Peace thy minister forever reign.
She has all charms affection to inspire—
Heart, warm with honesty and generous zeal;
Brain, strong to contrive and mighty to reveal;
Soul, full of teeming virtues. All outflow,
Blessings of joy and Love to free bestow.
Henceforth to guide us by thy loving arts,
We crown her sovereign in our heart of hearts.

TABLEAU.—*The Crowning of Peace.*

Dream Spirits.				*Attendants.*
QUEEN MAB.				RUBINA.
		GLORIA.		
		Bank.		
	INDUSTRY.	SERENA.	ART.	
MUSIC.				PLENTY.
R.				L.

SERENA *sits on bank,* C., *facing audience, hands folded across her breast.* GLORIA *stands behind her, placing the crown upon her head.* INDUSTRY R. *of* SERENA, *seated on bank, facing* R., *distaff in her left hand resting against shoulder.* ART *in the same positson* L. *of* SERENA, *facing* L., *with pallet in her left hand.* MUSIC *kneeling in front of* ART, *facing audience, playing upon lyre.* PLENTY *kneeling on right knee, front of* INDUSTRY, *outpouring her horn of plenty.* RUBINA, L., *back, with her attendants grouped behind her.* QUEEN MAB *enters,* R., *with her Dream Spirits, and group.*

All (repeat in concert).

On thee, O Freedom, grand and great!
   In confidence we lean,
Our land to bless, with fond caress,
   Of Happiness serene.
To hail thy crowning, gentle Peace,
   Let Music joyous soar,
While harvests wave and blessings lave
   Thy realm from shore to shore.

OUR CENTENNIAL.

The GENIUS OF UNIVERSAL PEACE *represented sitting upon a globe, the sceptre of authority in her hand, laurel wreath about her brow. Insignia. On either sides parties representing* AGRICULTURE, COMMERCE, MECHANIC ARTS, EDUCATION, MUSIC, ART. *Four* HERALDS *in front of these, two on each side.*

Genius of Universal Peace.

My council—ministers of human weal—
For your best offices I make appeal.
The world at peace, sheathed battle's direful brand,
With golden promise crowning every land;
The stains of bloody strife and bitter tears
Changed to sweet flowers, by chemistry of years,
And hate, subsided, stirs not by a breath
The air late dark with violence and death,—
Will ye not aid, by influence your own,
To plant Peace firmly on her regal throne,
That evermore unshaken it remain,
Without one spot its 'scutcheon fair to stain?
Men were not made to worry and to kill,
But a far nobler destiny to fill,
In which shall love and intellect combine,
On earth's great field, to soften and refine.

And yours the mission, in all lands displayed,
The car of Progress on its course to aid;
To give to Virtue grander power and zest
That may in ripened fulness manifest.
What say you, sisters of the Peaceful Muse?
Can you these offices of love refuse?

Agriculture.

My aim shall be to aid the cause of Peace,
My wish to bid all notes of discord cease,
And, in the *fields* of family or state,
The generous qualities to *cultivate*.
My *shares* are honest, in which men invest,
And never lose their consciences or rest.
Though hardened hands my votaries possess,
Their hearts are filled by thoughts of tenderness;
And e'en the seeds they on earth's bosom fling
React in good, and in their natures spring.
These on the side of Peace will e'er be found,
With Strife and Hatred never taking *ground*.

Commerce.

Be mine the duty peaceful claims to spread,
And beams of kindly interest to shed;
To lands remote fruits beneficial show
Of mutual intercourse from peace that flow;
O'er all the earth, through rough or kindly gales,
My flag shall float, and gleam my snowy sails;
Embodiment of missionary might,
I preach through trade, and spread the gospel light
That leads men, through necessity, to see
The need of each to each continually;
And thus for Peace—a paradox—maintain
Its blest dominion *ever*—in the *main*.

Mechanic Arts.

"My voice is *still* for war," and arts of Peace
Thrive 'neath my aiding with a grand increase.

For good of man I'm e'er on the alert,
His cup to fill, his evil to avert.
I bear him safely on the flying train;
I reap his barley, and I grind his grain;
I turn his spindles, print his daily news,
Sew up his garments, peg his boots and shoes.
In every circumstance of busy life
My hand is seen with benefaction rife.
True, when there's war I do a *little* aid
In killing off and maiming, I'm afraid;
But here I bid such recollection cease,
And pledge my best, and all I can, for Peace.

Education.

Be mine of sovereign Peace the loftiest praise!
We strive together fallen man to raise.
Mine is the province mental seed to sow;
Hers is the sun and dew to make it grow.
These, my fair temples, where they proudly rear
Their graceful turrets in the upper air,
Are citadels of Peace, 'gainst Ignorance
And Vice, to check them in their vile advance;
My banner on their walls, in pride unfurled,
The joy and admiration of the world!
Where men are wise, and honest judgment rules,
Is Education honored in her schools.
And Education, closest friend of Peace,
With a devotion that shall never cease,
Pledges its power to evermore maintain
The state and glory of her gentle reign.

Music.

Be mine the task to pour the joyous song
That may to Peace and her estate belong;
The "airs of peace," about which poets prate
Whene'er melodious horns they elevate.
Lo! all resources to the cause I lend
In one grand anthem to euphonious blend,

Till through the charmed channels of the air
Its note ecstatic is heard everywhere.
Sweet Melody shall do its level best,
And Harmony, sonorous, manifest,
Until the world delightedly shall see
Another Universal World's Peace Jubilee.

Art.

And mine the province kindly to restore
The fading glories that have gone before.
I give to Peace the trophies Valor won
On field of strife, when turbulence is done,
And the pale moon looks from the skies o'er-head
Upon the upturned faces of the dead.
I lay my offerings at her gracious feet,
And catch her smile of inspiration sweet,
Turning to win new glories for her trust,
And reappear in picture or in bust.
And glad to greet her, with a brimming heart
Will rush the mighty family of Art,
To do your bidding, honors meet to pay
To Peace, whose sceptre all the world doth sway.

Genius of Universal Peace.

Then let our heralds give our feeling voice,
And bid the world in halcyon peace rejoice;
Forgetting hate and sanguinary strife
In the amenities of peaceful life.
Here let the nations their productions bring,
For our fair shrine a fitting offering,
That, through a generous, emulative mood,
Each one may see another's greatest good.
Sound, Heralds of the North, South, East, and West,
This proclamation of our high behest.

(Cornet.) Herald of the North.

To the North's remotest home
Let these presents quickly come:

Hither bring your best increase,
Offering to sovereign Peace!

(Cornet.) Herald of the South.

Peoples of the Southern land,
Hear our sovereign's high command:
Bring the fruits of loom or vine
To adorn her sacred shrine.

(Cornet.) Herald of the East.

From the wealth of Orient clime
Bring meet tribute for the time,
On the altar grand to lay
Peace erects this happy day.

(Cornet.) Herald of the West.

From the West we bid you bring
Brain and nerve as offering,
Into wood and iron wrought,
With a nation's genius fraught.

The voice of the nations heard. The whole school in monotone saying,—

The mustering nations quickly wake to hear the welcome sound,
And o'er the seas and continents its stirring echoes bound;
From montain peak to mountain peak it wakes its glad acclaim,
With *Peace!* the burden of the tone, and *Peace!* the conquering name!
It swells, it swells exultantly on every human tongue,
And every breeze extends it, like a benediction flung;
The glory of its summons grand encircles sea and shore,
And hope takes heart that woe and strife shall curse the world no more.

Sweden (advances).

The North responds, and Sweden brings its gift,
A humble product of industrial thrift—
A few salt fishes, silver and copper ore,
An iron pig or so, and little more.

But, could we bring our glorious boreal lights,
That flash across the northern sky o' nights,
And the long twilights of the wintry days,
That follow on the sun's withholden rays,
No glory wrought of Art could rival ours,
Or speak for Peace with more exalted powers.

Russia (a boy costumed in fur advances).

Russia, the "Great Bear" of the frozen North,
Brings here for Peace his choicest treasures forth,
Leaving awhile his steppes for other climes,
And his sledge-bells for more mellifluous chimes.
Rough as the Russian air the gift he brings—
Hemp, needed where the guilty felon swings;
Duck,—canvas-back,—and cordage very strong,
And Russia leather,—not the penal thong;
Soap, linseed, fish, and wool, salt, wax, and honey,
And other useful articles for money.
Give Russia place. Substantial things are these
That she for honoring gentle Peace decrees.
Though he put on cold airs at times and storm,
Depend upon it, Russia's heart is warm.

Italy (advances).

Land of the olive and the teeming vine,
Italia brings her offering to the shrine;
Her fruits and grains, her silks of richest worth,
Her art, the pride and glory of the earth;
Coral and macaroni,—sea and soil,—
And sardines—"little fishes boiled in oil."
So much for Peace; and more she'd gladly bring
Upon the cairn of votive gifts to fling;
But more is really beyond her scope,
Unless she add a temporary pope.

Spain (advances).

Alas! poor Spain! but little can she bring
For such a scene as this an offering.

A little wine in which to quaff its health;
A little wool as sample of her wealth.
Her glory all has waned she had of yore,
To rest upon her palaces no Moor!
But yet a product she has lately grown,
That may for much that's lacking still atone:
Her people, tired of kingly rule and ban,
Have broke their bonds, and turned republican;
And this she brings, an offering more fine
Than baled merino or commercial wine.

Switzerland (advances).

To your appeal responds the land of Tell,—
Though some pretend he's but a myth, a sell;
But, if a myth, the people are not so,
Who have a world of "nick-nax" here to show—
Geneva watches, carving, jewelry,
Hand-organs,—on whose merits all agree,—
Toys for the babies, dolls as large as life,
And wooden plates for bread and carving-knife.
Not much for wealth and luxury; but, then,
We give the world a splendid line of men,
Who there amid our mountains have their birth,
Then, like our glacial streams, to bless go forth.
'Tis not in wealth that riches most are shown:
One AGASSIZ were worth a mint, alone.

France (advances).

What, room for France! Give her an ample space
In which to show her jewelry and lace,
Her silks unrivalled, and her Sevres wares,
Her tapestry, that imitation dares,
Her porcelains, without a flaw or fault,
Her claret, prunes, and truffles, wool, and salt;—
France, proudest of the European train,
That boasts of chivalry and Charlemagne!
Disliking lager, yet the German cup
Compelled to take and drink its contents up.

A bitter dose, but in it virtue lies;
For, like the housewife's yeast, 'twill make her rise,
Until, attaining old-time power again,
She'll reinstate her Alsace and Lorraine.

Germany (advances).

From her wide forests and her sunken mines
Germany kindly to this scene inclines.
She's had her fill of war, and beat her foe,
And now she'd fain in peaceful furrows sow.
She brings her tribute, from the loom and field,
Of cloths to which the whole world honor yield,
Of German iron and Germanic wine,
Of German toys and German music fine,
Of German silver that makes bright appeal,
But which thieves manage somehow not to steal.
She feels serene, her flag of warfare furled,
And cousin-german owns to all the world.
For competition here she brings her fruits,
And joins the ranks of Peace's proud recruits.

Austria (advances).

Make way for Austria, and her glittering ware
From fair Bohemia, beyond compare;
Her linen goods, her famous meerschaum pipes,
Her damasks of the most enchanted stripes;
Her gloves—assortment always kept on hand—
Her glauber salts—admired in every land!
Of Art the patron, Austria takes advance,
And for the palm would risk a friendly lance.
She brings her gifts the shrine of Peace to crown,
And with her loyalty gracefully comes down.

China (advances. Costume).

In broken China I my tongue surcease,
And say encouraging a word of Peace.
I pour my tea-cup to the very brim,
And drink the happiness and health of him.

Of Peace I say, he well doth pleasure me,
And suits my taste and fancy to one T.
How sweet to sit in peace, with tranquil eye,
Enjoying Oolong tea and chicken pie—
A four-legged chicken with a wiry tail—
Without a foe to worry or assail,
To threaten with an act injurious you,
Or bang your head, or cut quite off your queue.

India (advances. Veiled, dark gloves).

I am the dusky daughter of the sun,
Am " black, but comely "—see King Solomon—
And here would fain my offering outpour,
Meet tribute to this consecrated hour.
My camels, with their bulkiest of traps,
I've left below here at a livery chap's.
But here are shawls of exquisite design,
Wrought by the busy hands of maidens mine;
Here are rare gems and wealth of Orient pearls,
And graceful fabrics for your graceful girls,
Any of which, I think, would fitly pass
To decorate a graduating class.
Here are choice fruits of flavor most refined,
And flowers of every quality and kind.
My country's custom bids me not reveal
The face this modest drape doth thus conceal;
So, spare my blushes, and restrain your stares,
And judge my graces by my graceful wares.

England (advances. A boy dressed with top boots, if possible of burly make-up, broad-brimmed hat).

Look here, you know, just give me ample length
And breadth, and room according to my strength.
I always have an eye to peace, you know,
And make whate'er I can by doing so.
I'm peaceable myself, because it pays,
But money make of other people's frays—

Though I confess, with shame, to little wit
That by the Alabama I was bit.
I should have blustered free from that expense
If these Yanks hadn't forced me to the fence.
And I am bound in this grand scene, you know,
To make a great and overwhelming show,
And let the world see what John Bull can do,
If left his peaceful business to pursue.
I'll crowd your shelves with such rare merchandise,
That envy will enkindle in your eyes;
Dry goods, machinery, cutlery and slate,
Dyestuffs and chemicals, earthenware and plate.
As rich as Jason's most auriferous fleece
Are these, you know, the gifts I bring for Peace.

Brother Jonathan (heard whistling " Yankee Doodle" before he is seen, advances, dressed as the conventional Yankee, though not overdone, large black bag in his hand marked " Uncle Sam, City Hall, Boston").

So, *you've* all got here now, I guess *I'll* come,
And, with your leave, will make myself to hum.
I've got a carpet-bag of "notions" here,
To represent the western hemisphere,
Or the best part of it, without a doubt,
With Canada, *at present*, counted out. (*looking round*)
Well, this display does beat all natur, shore;
It seems jest like a Boston "dollar store.'
Sech heaps of things, and they're all well enough;
But we don't make sech ornamental stuff.
Our *eagle* isn't handsome, and can't sing,
But he has talons, and a mighty wing,
Which soars so far up in the azure sky,
That folks, even here, take hope to see him fly;
And so we, like our own imperial chick,
To usefulness far more than beauty stick;
Don't brag a bit, but let the world *find out*
Jest what the Yankee land has been about.

Perhaps these things are not so grand and bright,
But I'll bet high that you can't beat 'em quite;
Steam-engines, rat-traps, locomotives, schools,
Clothes-dryers, apple-pearers, farmers' tools,
Church organs, lemon-squeezers, stitch machines,
Pianos, gimlets, pots for baking beans,
Suspender buckles, nest-eggs, patent chair,
Varnish for boots, and garnish for the hair,
Et cetera—and so forth—*cetera*—
Enough to crowd your shanty, if you say.
Give me some place wherein to stow my traps,
And I'll not bother these ere fancy chaps;
Though some of 'em I hold in high respect,
From native admiration of the *sect*.
Now, hold on, France! don't elevate your nose
At my quaint talking and my quainter clo'es;
Remember, 'tis not by the dress alone
That what is called a *gentleman* is shown.
With us the genteel term is understood
When men are courteous, and kind, and good.
I've said my say. Please give my nick-nax shelves,
And they will speak in honor of themselves.

Genius of Universal Peace.

Welcome the whole, without a bound or stint,
Proclaimed with all the power of voice and print.
Here mingle kindly, thoughts and notes compare,
And in the feast of union each one share.
We give the meed of honor where 'tis due,
By arbitration liberal and true;
And from this scene, exalted and sublime,
Shall spread a glory lighting every clime.

The different nations shall then advance to the foot of the throne, and plant their banners at the feet of the Genius, the whole school singing,—

Live the dominion
  We crown to-day;
Peace spreads her pinion;
  Wide be her sway.
Pure the sky o'er us
  Smiles in its light;
Glad be our chorus
  This season bright.
Peace, gentle Peace,
  May she increase,
Her glory abound, and her reign never cease!

War's desolation,
  Father, we pray,
Spare every nation
  Here met to-day.
Prosper and bless them,
  Happy and free;
No ills distress them,
  Cherished by Thee.
Peace, gentle Peace,
  May she increase.
Her glory abound, and her reign never cease!

[Each young lady who personates a character can herself make a flag, representing her nationality, the material *im*material. The globe, or throne, can be very easily constructed of boards sawed and erected edge-wise, covered with cloth on which the geometrical lines are traced.

LOCHIEL'S WARNING.

[Lochiel, a Highland chieftain, while on his march to join the Pretender, is met by one of the Highland seers, or prophets, who warns him to return, and not incur the certain ruin which awaits the unfortunate prince and his followers, on the field of Culloden.]

Seer.

Lochiel, Lochiel, beware of the day
When the Lowlands shall meet thee in battle array!

For a field of the dead rushes red on my sight,
And the clans of Culloden are scattered in fight:
They rally, they bleed, for their country and crown!
Woe, woe, to the riders that trample them down!
Proud Cumberland prances, insulting the slain,
And their hoof-beaten bosoms are trod to the plain.
But hark! through the fast-flashing lightning of war,
What steed to the desert flies frantic and far?
'Tis thine, O Glenullin! whose bride shall await,
Like a love-lighted watch-fire, all night at the gate.
A steed comes at morning: no rider is there;
But its bridle is red with the sign of despair!
Weep, Albin! to death and captivity led!
O! weep! but thy tears cannot number the dead,
For a merciless sword on Culloden shall wave—
Culloden, that reeks with the blood of the brave!

Lochiel.

Go preach to the crowd, thou death-telling seer!
Or, if gory Culloden so dreadful appear,
Draw, dotard, around thy old wavering sight,
This mantle, to cover the phantoms of fright!

Seer.

Ha! laugh'st thou, Lochiel, my vision to scorn?
Proud bird of the mountain, thy plume shall be torn.
Say, rushed the bold eagle exultingly forth
From his home in the dark-rolling clouds of the North?
Lo! the death-shot of foemen out-speeding, he rode
Companionless, bearing destruction abroad;
But down let him stoop from his havoc on high!
Ah! home let him speed, for the spoiler is nigh.
Why flames the far summit? Why shoot to the blast
Those embers, like stars from the firmament cast?
'Tis the fire-shower of ruin, all dreadfully driven
From his eyrie, that beacons the darkness of heaven.
O, crested Lochiel! the peerless in might,
Whose banners arise on the battlements' height,

Heaven's fire is around thee, to blast and to burn;
Return to thy dwelling! all lonely return!
For the blackness of ashes shall mark where it stood,
And a wild mother scream o'er her famishing brood!

Lochiel.

False wizard, avaunt! I have marshalled my clan!
Their swords are a thousand—their bosoms are one!
They are true to the last of their blood and their breath,
And like reapers descend to the harvest of death.
Then welcome be Cumberland's steed to the shock!
Let him dash his proud foam like a wave on the rock!
But woe to his kindred and woe to his cause,
When Albin her claymore indignantly draws!
When her bonneted chieftains to victory crowd,
Clanranald the dauntless, and Moray the proud,
All plaided and plumed in their tartan array——

Seer.

Lochiel! Lochiel! beware of the day!
For, dark and despairing, my sight I may seal,
But man cannot cover what God would reveal.
'Tis the sunset of life gives me mystical lore,
And coming events cast their shadows before.
I tell thee, Culloden's dread echoes shall ring
With the bloodhounds that bark for thy fugitive king.
Lo! anointed by Heaven with the vials of wrath,
Behold, where he flies on his desolate path!
Now in darkness and billows he sweeps from my sight;
Rise! rise! ye wild tempests, and cover his flight!—
'Tis finished. Their thunders are hushed on the moors,
Culloden is lost, and my country deplores.
But where is the iron-bound prisoner? Where?
For the red eye of battle is shut in despair.
Say, mounts he the ocean-wave, banished, forlorn,
Like a limb from his country cast bleeding and torn?
Ah!. no; for a darker departure is near;
The war-drum is muffled, and black is the bier;

His death-bell is tolling. O! mercy, dispel
Yon sight, that it freezes my spirit to tell!
Life flutters, convulsed, in his quivering limbs,
And his blood-streaming nostril in agony swims!
Accursed be the fagots that blaze at his feet,
Where his heart shall be thrown ere it ceases to beat,
With the smoke of its ashes to poison the gale——

Lochiel.

Down, soothless insulter! I trust not the tale!
For never shall Albin a destiny meet
So black with dishonor, so foul with retreat.
Though my perishing ranks should be strewed in their gore
Like ocean-weeds heaped on the surf-beaten shore,
Lochiel, untainted by flight or by chains,
While the kindling of life in his bosom remains,
Shall victor exult, or in death be laid low,
With his back to the field, and his feet to the foe!
And, leaving in battle no blot on his name,
Look proudly to heaven from the death-bed of fame!

UNCLE SAM.

[For one male and two female characters.]

OLD FASHION *and* NEW FASHION *meeting (one dressed in the costume of '76 and the other as a modern belle.)*

Old Fashion. Well, I do declare! Sakes alive! What is this I see before me. (*turns* NEW FASHION *around*) A train, a bustle, and such a bonnet!

New Fashion. You seem to think I am dressed rather odd. Please look in the glass, ma'am, and criticise your own outlandish attire.

Old Fashion. Outlandish indeed! Why, this is the pink of fashion.

New Fashion. Yes, it might have been a hundred years since; but this is the prevailing style nowadays.

Old Fashion. What good is that little hat perched on your head like an old hen on a chimney?

New Fashion. And pray tell me if you think a bonnet big enough to take lodgings in so very becoming to your style of beauty. If you do, I don't.

Old Fashion. Don't be saucy, miss. In my days a young girl as pert as you was whipped and sent to bed.

New Fashion. And in my days an old woman like you would be shut up in a menagerie.

Old Fashion. You ought to be ashamed of yourself.

New Fashion. So had you.

Old Fashion. You're a saucy thing.

New Fashion. Ditto.

Enter UNCLE SAM.

Uncle Sam. Ladies, this is not exactly O. K. What's the row? I can't see two young damsels like you, fighting it out here on this line, without hitchin' in myself.

Old Fashion. She began it.

New Fashion. I didn't!

Old Fashion. You did!

New Fashion. She made fun of my dress.

Old Fashion. And quarreled with my bonnet.

New Fashion. She's ridiculous!

Old Fashion. There she goes again!

Uncle Sam. Stop! stop! Ladies, I insist. State your case, and I will decide upon its merits. Who speaks first?

Old Fashion. I, by the right of priority. In my day we used to go about in homespun, and were not ashamed of it—male and female.

Uncle Sam. Jest so!

Old Fashion. We hadn't the facilities nor the money to get ourselves up in these new-fangled fol-de-rols.

Uncle Sam. Jest so!

Old Fashion. We did the house work, and didn't go gadding about.

Uncle Sam. 'Spect you're right. Go ahead.

Old Fashion. We helped our mothers to do the chores.

Uncle Sam. I reckon.

Old Fashion. And we didn't care for style.

Uncle Sam. That's your side of the case. (*to* NEW FASHION) What do you wish to promulgate?

New Fashion. We don't wear homespun, for it's out of existence.

Uncle Sam. Jest so!

New Fashion. We have all the facilities to get ourselves up regardless.

Uncle Sam. Navigate.

New Fashion. As to the house work, if we don't do it, why somebody else does. In fact, Young America is entirely different from Old America in everything.

Uncle Sam. Except one.

New Fashion. What is that?

Uncle Sam. They both love Uncle Sam!

New Fashion. And the stars and stripes!

Old Fashion. And the American Eagle!

Uncle Sam. Now, Old Fashion and New Fashion, I beg of you to shake hands and be friends.

Old Fashion. With all my heart.

New Fashion. And mine. (*they shake hands.*)

Uncle Sam. Now, ladies, take my arm. (*they take his arm*) Gosh! I feel so proud! Two such pretty gals to tote around. I'm going to take you both to Philadelphia to my house,—called the Centennial. I'm going to introduce you to the whole world and the rest of creation. If they don't say you're the smartest, prettiest, cutest, chipperest pair of gals they ever laid eyes on, then you can call me an Ingin!

(*They go off walking very proudly.*)

THE SAILOR BOY'S RETURN.

[*For four boys*, JOHN, WILL, TOM, PAUL.]

Paul (*enters, dressed in sailor's costume*). Here, I am, safe and sound, after having served my country for three years. For that time I have undergone perils without number. Battles have I been in; but, strange to say, I have escaped without a scratch. Many a time has my heart leaped up to behold our starry banner flying at the peak! Often in foreign ports have I longed to see my home again; duty, whichever way I turned, stared me in the face and whispered, "Your country, my boy, before everything else!" How often have I dreamed of the dear ones at home—sisters and brothers, and last, though not least, my father and mother. I have received no letter from them for the last year. I wonder how they all are! In coming up from town I heard that they were all alive. How I long to see them. There's mother with her dear soft eyes and kindly smile. There's father with his ever-welcome words, and sister, the household pet. Then come my three brothers, Tom, Will, and John. Many a time I have thought of them as I tossed about on the raging seas. I wonder if they have thought as much of me? How willful I was to run away to sea. But they would not let me go to fight for the dear old flag, and so I went without their consent. It was wrong, I know, and bitterly has my conscience tortured me for my error. As I live, here come my three brothers, sauntering down the lane. Let me keep out of sight and surprise them. (*goes off to one side.*)

Enter WILL, TOM, *and* JOHN.

Will. As you say, Tom, in these times I think it is the duty of everybody, man and boy, to do the best in his power for the welfare of his native land.

Tom. That's so; think of what our native land has done for us. Our country is our second mother. She has protected us, taught us, and nurtured us, and we would be basely ungrateful to turn aside when she needs our services.

John. I should like to be where our dear brother Paul is. He ran away from home to help fight the battles of his country, and I should like to do the same.

Tom. But would that be doing our duty to our parents?

Will. They say we are too young to go.

Tom. And they know best.

John. How I should long to sail the seas, and strike my feeble blow in defence of the flag!

Tom. Let us run away like Paul did.

Will. It would break mother's heart. See how she has mourned over our Paul. Why, she has not heard a word from him in a year, although she has written repeatedly.

John. I should like to go; but something tells it would be wrong.

Tom. Think of the honor we should gain.

Will. Think of the weeping ones at home.

John. Think of the flag in peril.

Tom. I shall go for one!

Will. I will join you, Tom!

John. Boys, I think you will have to take me along!

Tom. Let us arrange matters. We will go quietly home, as if nothing unusual were the matter. We will collect all the clothes we need, and meet at this place about dusk. Then good-bye to this dull place, and hie for honor and glory!

John. Hurrah!

Will (tossing his hat). Hurrah!

Tom. Let me see! how much money can we raise between us?

John. I have a dollar.

Will. And I.

Tom. And I have two. That will pay our way to the navy yard, I think. Then we can write home, and calm the fears of mother and father and sister.

John. Many a great admiral ran away from home.

Will. True. Mothers are so careful of their boys.

Tom. What should we do if they were not?

John. Who denies that? But, boys, remember, at dusk to-night.

Tom. I shall be here.

Will. And I.

John. Who knows, perhaps we shall meet our dear brother Paul. (PAUL *comes from his hiding place.*)

Paul. You needn't go far to do that! Don't you know me boys?

Tom. Paul!

John. Brother Paul!

Will. Did you spring from the earth?

Paul (*embracing them*). Safe at home, boys! Safe and sound. The war is all over, too! So you were about to follow my example and run away, were you? Fie, for shame. I did a coward's action, although I mistook it for one of great bravery. It was my place to obey my father and mother, and bitterly have I repented. Although I loved my country and would lay down my life for her, yet I could have served her here at home, if it were against the wishes of the dear ones at home. But I know they will forgive me.

Tom. Yes, indeed, Paul. They honor you now for your patriotism.

Paul. I am longing to see them. Hurrah, the war is over! No more fighting! No more running away, boys.

Tom. We were only about to follow your illustrious example.

Paul. I am glad I overheard you, and spoiled your project.

Will. Three cheers for sailor Paul!

Tom.
John. } Hip, hip, hurrah, hurrah, hurrah!

Paul. And, boys, allow me to propose three cheers for the stars and stripes, and may the old flag wave forever!

All. Hurrah! hurrah! hurrah! (*Exeunt.*)

A CENTENNIAL DRAMA.

MRS. E. D. CHENEY.

SCENE.—*A country town near Boston.* PERIOD—1775.

CHARACTERS.

GEN. WASHINGTON.—Old Continental costume.
MR. BAXTER, a Tory.—Old-fashioned full dress.
HENRY BRADFORD, a young soldier.—Soldier's costume.
ZEKE and NAT, soldiers.—Countrymen's dress, with some attempt at soldier's dress.
MOLL PITCHER, a sibyl.—Red cloak, dark skirt, hat and straight feather, staff.
MRS. BAXTER, a female Tory.—Full dress, old style.
GRACE, their supposed daughter.—Blue dress, simple and pretty.
MRS. BRADFORD.—Plain, nice widow's dress.
Soldiers, Young Girls, General's Aides.

SCENE I.—*A green in front of* Mr. Baxter's *house.* Grace *sitting on a bench or bank.*

Enter Moll Pitcher.

Grace. O! my dear good Molly, say,
 Is my lover brave and true?
Moll. As the sun is to the day
 Is your lover unto you.
 But, maiden, are you brave and strong?
 For a struggle comes ere long.
 If a higher duty call,
 Will you bid him give up all,
 Even your love?
Grace. Ah! my heart,
 Can it be that we must part?
Moll. Tell me, maiden, are you true
 To your country?
Grace. Hush! to you
 I may confess. I'm no Tory.
 But my father, hard and stern,
 Nor my mother, must not learn
 That I help the patriot band
 With my heart and with my hand,
 Praying daily for their glory.
Moll. Hark, then: soon a struggle comes—
 In the air I hear the drums.

Enter Mr. Baxter.

Mr. B. You here, old witch? I'll have you hung
 For your vile, mischievous tongue.
 (*to* Grace) Away, you minx! your needle mind,
 And don't be prating here.
 (*to* Moll) You beldam, go, or much I fear
 The ducking-pond you'll find.
Moll. Proud fool! you cannot make me bend,
 Or own your haughty power,

Which, like your king, shall shortly end—
Quick comes the fatal hour.
(*half chanting*) The swords shall cross,
The blood shall flow,
And England's mighty power lie low.

Mr. B. What mean you, witch? Now, by my life—
(*aside*) O, dear! methinks I hear my wife.

Enter MRS. BAXTER.

Mrs. B. Pray, sir, why do you speak so loud?
I thought you must harangue a crowd.
Who is this woman?

Mr. B. O, my dear,
Don't blame me.

Mrs. B. Speak out, sir. I fear
You plot some mischief. (*to* MOLL) Who are you?

Moll. One to whom the past and the future are known;
One to whom sorrow and blessings are shown;
Who readeth your riddle, and knows why the wife
Rules over the husband.

Mrs. B. O, hush! on your life!
Here's money—quick! Leave me; the child must not
know.

Moll. (*refuses money*). No, madam! but listen, before I will go,
This fate I must speak: No honor to you can there
come;
No luck to your child, and no peace to your home,
Till the red-coat shall yield to the Red, White, and Blue,
And the loving and loyal shall wed with the true.
(*Exit* MOLL.)

Mrs. B. (*aside*). Ah! if Grace should know that she is not our
child,
And the fortune is hers, I should die or go wild.
(*Exit* MR. *and* MRS. BAXTER.)

Enter HENRY BRADFORD.

Henry. Darling Grace, I'm loth to grieve you,
But I fear that I must leave you.

Grace. Leave me, dearest? Say not so;
　　　　Let me follow where you go.
Henry. Hark! a secret: To-night the patriots will
　　　　Encamp on and fortify Bunker Hill.
　　　　I must be there with my followers brave,
　　　　I must be there my country to save,—
　　　　To conquer or fill up a true soldier's grave.
Grace. O! Henry, my lover, this deed will you dare?
　　　　And I can do nothing but give you my prayer.
　　　　But my heart and my love shall be with you there.

　　　　　　Enter Mr. Baxter.

Mr. B. How—you rascal, rebel sneak!—
　　　　Dare you to my daughter speak?
　　　　She is not for such as you.
Henry. Sir! my love for her is true,
　　　　And I pray you bless her choice.
Mr. B. No, sir. I will give my voice
　　　　Only to a soldier brave,
　　　　Loyal to his rightful king. 　　　　　(*Exit.*)
Henry. Ah! we must the country save,
　　　　Though our joy it may not bring.
　　　　We must be true
　　　　To the Red, White, and Blue.

　　　　　　Music, "*Yankee Doodle.*"

　　　　Hark to that noise!
　　　　Yes, my brave boys
　　　　Are calling for me.
Grace. O, let them come in, that I may bless
　　　　The banner bright for which you fight.

Enter Soldiers *with banner and drums, and playing "Yankee Doodle."* Grace *goes and shakes hands with them, then takes off a blue scarf and binds it about the drum.*

　　　　As true as the blue,
　　　　And as pure as the white,

    And as brave as the red,
     May you go to the fight.

     Enter MOLL.

  I bless the banner and bless the cause;
  Fight for your country, her freedom and laws;
  And when you have driven the foe from the track,
  Your mothers and maidens shall welcome you back.
Zeke. Well, Captain Henry, we'll all fight,
  With such a pretty girl to bless the right.
Nat. And blessing will come with old Molly's good will,
  So gladly we'll march to defend the old hill.

   Enter MR. *and* MRS. BAXTER.

Mr. B. What the fiend is this all about?
  You rebel rascal—take your men out!
  At the first fire of King George's gun
  The question will be how fast they can run.
Grace. No, father, no; they are brave and true.
Mr. B. You impudent girl, what's that to you?
Moll. Beware, old tyrant, to her what you say!
  She'll be prouder and higher than you some day.
Mr. B. Hush! hush! Good Molly, not a word!
Grace. What is this strange speech I've heard?
Mrs. B. Silence, you fool! let her triumph to-day.
  Her rash young fool will be soon out of the way,
  And then it will be our turn for the play.

SOLDIERS *form and march off.* HENRY *takes a silent farewe.. of* GRACE, *and puts himself at their head. Curtain falls.*

SCENE II.—*After the battle. Same green—or a room in* MR. BAXTER's *house.* MR. *and* MRS. BAXTER *and* GRACE.

Mrs. B. My child, this British colonel woos you;
  No nobler suitor e'er will choose you;

	He'll take you to his English home
	Of splendor.
Grace.	I will not come.
	My heart is here, O mother dear,
	With my poor wounded hero.
Mrs. B.	O, foolish girl!
	These feeble bands that sought the fight,
	And quailed before King George's might,
	Will all be scattered. He will die,
	Or else be forced from home to fly.
Grace.	Then I'll go with him, well or ill.
Mr. B.	No, girl! I am your father still.
	You won't be free for many a day,
	And by my right I'll bar the way.
	Consent to wed as I've declared,
	Or I'll hold you under watch and ward.

Enter MOLL.

Moll.	You will, O vilest man of men!
	Have you forgotten Moll Pitcher, then?
Grace.	O, good woman, tell me, pray,
	Aught that may my heart relieve,
	Else 'twill surely break to-day,
	So for Henry do I grieve.
Moll.	You are not the child of this cruel pair,
	But your father was brave and your mother was fair.
	The blood of old Plymouth ran in his veins,
	A fortune he gathered by labor and pains,
	And dying he left you in charge to this friend,
	Who claims you his child, to the end
	He may seize on your fortune; but I loved him well,
	And I've watched o'er his child that this tale I might tell.
Mrs. B.	} O, she is crazy, don't believe her.
Mr. B.	
Moll.	No, you can no more deceive her.
	The right will stand.
	(*to* GRACE) Your father's dying hand

| | Gave me this ring.
| | (*to* Mr. *and* Mrs. Baxter) To you I'll bring
| | Full many a proof
| | I speak the truth.
Mr. B.   Nay! nay! good Molly, we can't deny
           The tale you tell, and will not try.
           We sought her good.
Mrs. B.   Hush, hush, old fool!
           Your hasty tongue and temper school.
           (*to* Moll) We sought our own, and hoped when grown
           To woman's age, to wed her far away,
           And keep her fortune; but, ah me! to-day
           Our plots are vain. Forgive me, child, I pray.
Mr. B.   I am her guardian, and she must obey.
           For two years yet I can her rule.
Mrs. B. You rule a woman, you stupid fool?
           You'd better coax her to hush up this story.
Grace.   I will, when you cease to act as a Tory.
           If you'll give your consent I shall be Henry's wife,
           And will join the good cause. I'll support you thro' life.
Moll.   Grant it, or to-morrow morn
           Of wealth and honor you'll be shorn.
Mrs. B. O noble maiden, we grant all you say,
           And feel freer in heart than for many a day;
           For ill-gotten plunder will never succeed,
           And who fights 'gainst his country is wretched indeed.
                              (*Curtain falls.*)

SCENE III.—*A room in* Henry's *mother's house.* Henry, *pale and languid, lying on couch, his mother sits at his head. Young girls sewing, spinning, and weaving.*

Mother. Ah, my poor boy! will you never revive?
          I'd give up my life if you only might live.
          Why should you despair! Our defeat on the hill
          Was a triumph—our men gather still;
          And hark you, they say
          The commander-in-chief will be with them to-day.

Henry. And here I lie,
But I must try
At least to die
Where every brave man ought to lie—
Upon the battle field.
I will not to the British yield.
But O, my heart!
I could have died without a groan
Upon the battle-field alone
Had Grace been true.
That she could leave me,
That she could treacherously deceive me,
To wed her country's foe,
Is harder than the hireling's blow.
But, sisters dear, who patient weave
The thread, to clothe our soldiers brave,
You teach me all my strength to save
And to my country's cause to cleave.
Let me lean on you, mother dear;
I'll walk a little. (*rises and walks, supported by his mother.*)

Enter ZEKE.

Zeke, you here!

Zeke. O, Captain Henry, you must get well.
The troops are mustering everywhere.
Let old Moll Pitcher try her spell,
And the blessed old parson put up a prayer.

Enter MOLL.

Yes, my hero, young and brave,
Cast this wretched gloom away.
Rise, your country's cause to save,
Washington comes here to-day.

All (*exclaim*). Washington, our noble chief!
We will serve him night and day. (HENRY *lies down.*)

Enter GRACE.

Grace. Mother, where is Henry dear?
         O, what struggles I have known!
         Harassed by each bitter fear,
         In my chamber dark and lone;
         For my cruel father held me there,
         And would not answer to my prayer,
         Till this true and noble friend
         (*to* MOLL) Came her powerful aid to lend.
Henry. 'Tis her voice! What have I heard?
         Can I trust this blessed word!
         Grace, my darling, are you true?
Grace. How could I be false to you,
         Whom I love more than my life?
Henry. O, my joy, my love, my wife.
         Mother, I am strong again:
         I feel no wounds, I know no pain,
         I am strengthened by your word.
         (*to* ZEKE) Brave fellow, bring me my musket and sword;
         Let the drum beat, I am ready to fight.
         Grace, though I leave you,
         I'll never deceive you;
         We are wedded for life,
         And are one in the strife
         For the true and the right.
         Call in the boys. I long to see
         The trusty men who follow me.

Enter SOLDIERS.

First Soldier. Hurrah! for our captain so noble and high.
Second Soldier. Hurrah! for the women so trusty and true.
Third Soldier. Hurrah! for the girls for whom gladly we'd die.
All. Hurrah! one and all, for the red, white, and blue.

Enter MR. *and* MRS. BAXTER.

Mrs. B. Neighbors, we ask your pardon all,
         If we have seemed both hard and stern,
         We have found King George is in the wrong,
         Which proves that we may live and learn.

Mr. B.   This loving pair,
        We fondly bless,
        And wish them health
        And happiness.
Zeke.   Hark! hark! I hear a drumming:
        Listen—Washington is coming?

      Enter WASHINGTON, *with Aides, etc.*

Washington. Good friends, I'm glad to greet you all
        Here, ready for your country's call.
        Our cause needs all the men to fight,
        The women working for the right.
        With men so brave, with girls so true,
        We cannot fail—I pledge my life to you!
All.   And ours to you with heart and hand.
Moll.   God bless this noble patriot band!
        The flame that rose on Bunker Hill
        Shall glow and blaze until it fill
        Our glorious land from shore to shore,
        And Freedom's mighty song shall rise
        Free and triumphant to the skies.
        And when a hundred years are o'er,
        Its mighty echoes shall be heard;
        And men and women gather still
        About the base of Bunker Hill,
        To tell again the old, old story
        Of Washington and all our glory—
        To wave again the flag so true,
        The stars above—red, white, and blue.
        But then not war, but peace shall claim
        The brightest crown, the dearest name,
        And England claim her mighty son
        As owing birth to her alone;
        And North and South, and West and East,
        Shall all unite in Freedom's feast,
        And with loud cheers of right good will,
        Hail to the day of Bunker Hill!

      Tableau. Song, "Hail Columbia." Curtain falls.

AMERICA'S BIRTHDAY PARTY.

GEORGE B. BARTLETT.

CHARACTERS.

AMERICA.—Blue waist trimmed with gilt paper stars, skirt made of flags; a pointed crown of blue paper with golden stars. She stands upon a table draped with flags, and leans with her left hand upon a tall staff surmounted by a liberty cap. The other characters stand in a semi-circle around her. Each advances to the centre as she speaks or sings, and kneels before AMERICA and presents her gift, then retires to her place. AMERICA acknowledges each present, which she places on a small table at her side.

INDUSTRY.—Long brown robe. Gift, horn of plenty.
AGRICULTURE.—Long green robe. Gift, sheaf of wheat.
ELECTRICITY.—Long red robe. Gift, coil of wire.
SCIENCE.—Long black robe. Gift, a map.
WEALTH.—Long yellow robe. Gift, casket of jewels.
LITERATURE.—Dark blue robe. Gift, roll of manuscript.
COMMERCE.—Light blue robe, trimmed with cotton wadding. Gift, a ship.
INTEGRITY.—Long white robe. She presents no gift.

All join in singing, to the tune of "Auld Lang Syne," this opening chorus:

A hundred years have swiftly rolled in endless round away,
Since our beloved country first beheld the light of day;
And now we bring as birthday gifts our choicest treasures here,
To celebrate the glorious Fourth and this Centennial year.

America.

Beloved ones! with joy I see your smiling faces here,
And listen to your full report of each progressive year.
Stand forth and tell what each has done, my children strong and true—
Industry! as your time is short, suppose we hear from you.

Industry.

Where the primeval forest stood a thousand cities rise;
Ten thousand churches upward point in warning to the skies;

Millions of looms are weaving fast with tireless, rapid hands;
Railroads now bind the continent with solid iron bands.

Agriculture.

I've made the howling wilderness to blossom as the rose;
Where once the sand blew hot and fierce the wheat now freely grows;
And cattle, from the western plains, go forth in herds to feed
The hungry poor in distant lands, wherever there is need.

Electricity.

I've placed a girdle round the world, and underneath the deep;
Without regard to time or space, from pole to pole I leap;
The darkest places of the world now shine with flashing light,
And, more than all of this, in truth, I've learned to read and write.

Science.

All things on earth and in the air I measure, small and great;
The orbits of the starry hosts with ease I calculate;
I heal the sick, and teach the wise, and banish every pain;
And things that seemed a useless waste I bring to use again.

Wealth.

From California's golden shore to realms of crystal ice,
The nations multiply their gains by taking my advice;
Your bonds are known in every land, and treasured near and far,
And by the next Centennial year your bills may be at par.

Literature.

New books are published every day, some worthy of the name;
Our authors now in foreign lands are slowly getting fame;
Our magazines are wide awake, the children's joy and pride;
Our schools the best the sun can see in all his journey wide.

Commerce.

Our flag now floats in every breeze, our prows all waves divide;
Our goods are sent to every land, and scattered far and wide;
We gather gems from Afric's shores, where golden torrents roll,
And oil from where the freezing waves defend the northern pole.

America.

I hear with joy your welcome words of faithful duty done,
But in your noble company I see a silent one.
Approach, my dearest, purest child, and fearlessly proclaim
The progress made by honest truth, the best-enduring fame.

Integrity.

Alas! I sadly must confess my labors are in vain,—
For public men too often fall before the greed of gain;
The thirst for fame has been too much for many a noble soul,
And self, of many a patriot heart, has gained the full control.

America.

With sorrow and distress I hear this story, sad, but true,—
But next Centennial year shall be a brighter one for you;
The faithless ones shall bow in dust before your warning voice,
And our next set of public men shall make your heart rejoice.

All kneel before AMERICA *and sing the closing chorus.*

We hail the age of truth and right, when patriots shall be
Like those of old, from selfish aims and low ambitions free;
And truth and progress onward go, forever hand in hand,
And our beloved country make the greatest, purest land.

NOTE.—These verses can be spoken, if preferred, singing only the opening and closing chorus.

COLUMBIA'S DAUGHTERS.

JOHN KEYNTON.

[*For a flag raising.*]

MASSACHUSETTS *and* VIRGINIA, *meeting.*

Massachusetts.
Well, there, Virginia, who would think to meet
You here so early, looking smart and sweet?

Virginia.

Why, sister Massachusetts, I'm on hand
To take my part this day so proud and grand.
You know that in the past we labored side by side,
And the name and fame of Washington
Was Massachusetts' pride.
Thy sister's heart with pride will ever thrill
When Warren's name is mentioned,
And grand old Bunker Hill.

Massachusetts.

True, sister dear, our sons fought side by side,
Yorktown and Concord must ever be allied.
Your Washington and Jefferson, and all the brilliant throng,
Though born upon your virgin soil, to us as well belong.
But here come sisters New Hampshire and the rest,
Thirteen in all; make each a welcome guest.

The remainder of the original Thirteen States appropriately dressed in white with red and blue scarfs, bearing a shield, upon which is the name of the State they represent, here enter and take their appropriate place upon the platform.

Rhode Island.

Though I'm the smallest State in all the lot
Yet I, good sisters, must not be forgot.
My sons on many a well-contested field
Have nobly fought, and been the last to yield!
Therefore, my sisters, on this festal day
Let me unite with you in sisterly array.

New York.

Brave little Rhody, we'll take care of you
Along with old Connecticut, forever staunch and true;
We welcome you as proudly as did our sires of old
Our patriot sires of " '76 " when the din of battle rolled!

New Hampshire.

Here's North and South Carolina, as I live,
To each of them a loving welcome give;

For Marion's name and Sumpter's still will shine,
Both in our hearts forever we enshrine.

New Jersey.

Georgia, Delaware, and Maryland here are seen,
With proud old Pennsylvania—*the whole Thirteen.*
Thrice welcome, sisters, in your grand array,
We greet you all upon our natal day.
Each one is proud of what her sons have done,
On history's page still shines the fame they've won.
Monmonth and Saratoga, Trenton and Valley Forge,
Mad old Wayne at Stony Point leaps up its rocky gorge,
Unfurls the flag, and on its ramparts proudly sets
Our symbol stars, whose radiant beams no sister e'er forgets.

Maryland (pointing to flag).

Hail sacred flag, to sons of Freedom dear,
Our Country's valor reared thine honors here.
Eternal blessings crown thy rich increase,
Thy *bands* of *Union,* and thy *stars* of *Peace.*
In years gone by amid the iron hail
My sons upheld thee; thy stars shall never pale;
Upon my wave-washed shore was found
A spot where God could be adored—around
Whose altars Freedom, Happiness and Peace
Could linger, blest with large increase.
Hail, blest asylum! happy country, hail!
O'er thee may truth and virtue, but never foe, prevail.

Pennsylvania.

I come, dear sisters, this Centennial year to bring
A hearty welcome, for around us fondly cling
The dearest memories. "Our Bell of Liberty" sublime
Peals forth to-day as grand a strain as in the olden time;
Upon my soil, a century ago, this very day,
The truth was told with bated breath, that flew on winds away.
Our UNION then was born; the assurance then was given
That a new star in the firmament of Freedom had arisen,
Whose light for ever more should shine upon our history's pages,
The symbol bright of Hope and Fame throughout the endless ages.

Connecticut (pointing).

But, sisters, see Columbia fair appears,
Crowned with her radiant diadem of stars.

Georgia.

Her brow is laurelled with a hundred years;
Young Neptune stands upon her right—upon her left old Mars.

Delaware.

A song of welcome let us sing,
The joyous notes prolong;

North Carolina.

Our voices on the air shall ring,
And this shall be our song.

South Carolina (advances to the front and sings).

Columbia, the gem of the ocean!
The home of the brave and the free!
The shrine of each Patriot's devotion,
A world offers homage to thee;
Thy mandates make heroes assemble,
When Liberty's form stands in view,
Thy banners make Tyranny tremble,
When borne by the Red, White and Blue.
When borne by the Red, White and Blue,
When borne by the Red, White and Blue,
Thy banners make Tyranny tremble
When borne by the Red, White and Blue.

COLUMBIA *here enters, attended on the right by a sailor and on the left by a soldier. The remaining States group appropriately.*

South Carolina (sings).

Ye sons of Columbia, come hither,
And join in our songs of delight,
May the wreath you have worn never wither,
May the stars of your glory grow bright;

May the service united ne'er sever,
But hold to their colors so true,
The *Army* and *Navy* forever,
Three cheers for the Red, White and Blue.
    Three cheers for the Red, White and Blue,
    Three cheers for the Red, White and Blue,
    The Army and Navy forever,
    Three cheers for the Red, White and Blue.

South Carolina.

Thrice welcome, sister, brave in peace and war,
Thrice welcome! and there's room for many more!
Though older sisters, yet our love's the same,
With you we link our heritage and fame;
DIVIDED once, oh weak is our alliance!
UNITED, we can bid the world defiance!

All repeat slowly in concert

Our Country! 'tis a glorious land!
With broad arms stretched from shore to shore,
The proud Pacific chafes her strand,
She hears the dark Atlantic roar;
And nurtured on her ample breast,
Now many a goodly prospect lies
In Nature's noblest grandeur drest,
Enamelled with a thousand dyes.
Great God! we thank thee for this home,
This bounteous birth-land of the free,
Where wanderers from afar may come,
And breathe the air of liberty!
Still may her flowers untrampled spring,
Her harvests wave, her cities rise,
And yet, till time shall fold her wing,
Remain Earth's loveliest paradise.

Columbia.

Welcome, daughters, brave and fair and true,
As welcome as to flowers the morning dew:
We meet to celebrate the glorious morn,
When Liberty, sweet Liberty was born.

A little child she was, long, long ago,
'Twas you who fostered her and marked her grow;
Your hands first wove the precious flag I bear,
Your sons upheld it midst the battle's glare,
This banner, with its bright and starry field.
To FRIENDS we give—to FOES we *never* yield!
This flag we bring in fair Columbia's name,
Our stars and stripes—bright emblem of her fame!
Unto the breeze its folds are now unfurled,
And 'neath its stars we greet the *new-born world!*
Our fathers in the dim and shadowy past
Fought, bled and died—their lives and fortunes cast
Into the scale—that we this natal year
Might on this spot a glorious shrine uprear
To Liberty, where pilgrims from distant lands might come
And with Columbia's sons and daughters,
The air of Freedom breathe,
And quaff its life-renewing waters!
One hundred years have come and gone
Since first the truth was told,
That Man was to the King an equal born!
This truth to-day we firmly hold!
God bless the name of Washington,
And may his sacred fame
Linked with that of Jefferson,
Imperishable remain!

To the committee receiving the flag.

Accept this flag, the gift of hands so fair,
Long may it stream upon the sunny air!
Proud be its march upon the land and sea,
The emblem of our Country's Liberty!
Upon the field each State hath wrought its star—
Let no rude hand its bright effulgence mar!
And, in the future, may it brightly shine,
More radiant glowing with the lapse of time,
And when another natal day shall come,
Oh, may our land still be bright Freedom's home!

To the States.

Fair daughters! now forever great and free,
This be our song—" The Emblem of our Liberty,"
And may its strains, so resonant and grand,
Be long the anthem of our native land!

All sing (AIR—" *Viva l' America.*")

Unfurl our standard of stars to the breeze,
Still may it flutter o'er land and o'er seas;
Our flag we'll honor till our latest breath,
    Shield and defend it till death.
Long as the stars in the welkin shall shine,
Honor, and Freedom, and Beauty be thine.
Float thou forever, o'er land and o'er sea,
    Emblem of fair purity.
Hurrah for our flag, the flag of the free!
The flag of our Fathers, our banner shall be;
Long may it wave o'er land and o'er sea,
    Symbol of sweet Liberty.

Emblem thou art of the good and the true,
Heaven-born banner of Red, White and Blue;
Still we'll protect thee from tyrannous scars,
    Rallying here 'neath thy stars.
North and South meet this jubilee day,
And with the East our bright ensign display,
Proudly the West joins the jubilant strain,
    Brothers united again.
        Hurrah for our flag, etc.

Flag of our Fathers! the Blue of thy field,
With the White and the Red forever shall shield
Millions of earth-born, who shall in thy name
    Kinship and brotherhood claim.
God still our Union protect and defend,
Thy choicest blessing forever extend;

Make of our land in the future to be
   A refuge where all shall be free.
      Hurrah for our flag, etc.

God of our fathers! to thee sounds our cry,
Echoed by millions to Thy throne on high,
Strengthen our Union and prosper our land,
   Make us as brothers to stand!
Still humbly bending to Thee we would pray
That thou, in Thy wisdom, may'st speed the day
When all the wide world in our flag shall see
   The symbol of their liberty.
Hurrah for our flag, the flag of the free!
The flag of our fathers our banner shall be;
Long may it float o'er land and o'er sea,
   Symbol of their liberty.

Old MOTHER COLONY *addresses* COLUMBIA.

A glorious shrine thou hast upreared,
Where once the savage trod.
The Pilot who has safely steered
Thy " Ship of State " is God ;
'Tis He who has so prospered thee,
And to thy daughters given
This glorious banner of the free,
Whose hues were born in heaven.
God's blessed book let each child read,
Its teachings never scorn,
Its precepts they must ever heed,
If they would breast the storm.
"In God we trust"—this motto be
The watchword and the sign,
And peoples yet unborn shall see
Thy stars more brightly shine.

New York (*advances to front of platform*).

When Freedom from her mountain height
Unfurled her standard to the air,

She tore the azure robe of night,
And set the stars of glory there;
She mingled with its gorgeous dyes
The milky baldric of the skies,
And striped its pure celestial white
With streakings of the morning light;
Then from his mansion in the sun
She called her eagle-bearer down,
And gave into his mighty hand
The symbol of her chosen land.
Majestic monarch of the cloud!
Who rear'st aloft thy regal form,
To hear the tempest-trumpings loud,
And see the lightning lances driven,
Where strive the warriors of the storm,
And rolls the thunder drum of heaven—
Child of the sun! to thee 'tis given
To guard the banner of the free,
To hover in the sulphur smoke,
To ward away the battle stroke,
And bid its blendings shine afar,
Like rainbows on the cloud of war,
The harbinger of victory!
Flag of the brave! thy folds shall fly
The sign of hope and triumph high,
When speaks the signal trumpet tone,
And the long line comes gleaming on.
Ere yet the life-blood, warm and wet,
Had dimmed the glistening bayonet,
Each soldier's eye shall brightly turn
To where thy sky-born glories burn;
And, as his springing steps advance,
Catch war and vengeance from the glance;
And when the cannon mouthings loud
Heave in wild wreaths the battle shroud,
And gory sabres rise and fall,
Like shoots of flame on midnight's pall,
There shall thy meteor glances glow,

And cowering foes shall sink beneath
Each gallant arm that strikes below
That lovely messenger of death.
Flag of the seas! on ocean wave
Thy stars shall glitter o'er the brave;
When Death careening on the gale,
Sweeps darkly around the bellied sail,
And frighted waves rush wildly back
Before the broadside's reeling rack,
Each dying wanderer of the sea
Shall look at once to heaven and thee,
And smile to see thy splendors fly
In triumph o'er his closing eye.
Flag of the free hearts hope and home,
By angel hands to valor given!
Thy stars have lit the welkin dome,
And all thy hues were born in heaven.
Forever float that standard sheet!
Where breathes the foe but falls before us,
With Freedom's soil beneath our feet,
And Freedom's banner waving o'er us.

All repeat in concert.

Forever float that standard sheet!
Where breathes the foe but falls before us,
With Freedom's soil beneath our feet,
And Freedom's banner waving o'er us.

After COLUMBIA *and her daughters have left the platform,* MIN-
NEHAHA *advances and thus soliloquizes:*

Minnehaha.

Westward, westward, further westward,
Oh, my people, to the sunset,
Go into the purple shadows,
From the rising sun go westward:
Like the new moon slowly, slowly
Sinking in the purple distance.
Farewell! farewell! Oh, my people,

We must leave our sparkling waters,
Our green fields and waving cornfields,
And our forests dark and lonely.
Gitchie Manitou, the Mighty,
The Great Spirit—the Creator
Sent a message in a vision,
Of the greatness of the stranger;
And he spake to me in this wise:
Minnehaha—Laughing Water,
Take your people further westward,
In the dim and purple distance
Where the sunset lingers longest.
You must go there with your people,
For the strong and mighty white man
Your old hunting ground inhabits,
And from many, many wigwams
Smoke curls up in cloudy vapors.
Thus beheld I, in my vision ;
"All the secrets of the future—
Of the distant days that shall be.
I beheld the westward marches
Of the unknown crowded nations.
All the land was full of people,
Restless, struggling, toiling, striving,
Speaking many tongues, yet feeling
But one heart beat in their bosoms.
In the woodlands rang their axes,
Smoked their towns in all the valleys ;
Over all the lakes and rivers
Rushed their great canoes of thunder.
Then a darker, drearier vision
Passed before me. I beheld your nation scattered,
Weakened, warring with each other;
Saw the remnants of our people
Like the withered leaves of Autumn
Scattered." So, my people, further westward,
This alone remains unto us.
We must say unto the white man,

Spare to us and to our children —
Spare to us one little corner
In the distant land of sunset,
Where our wives and little children
Can sit down beneath the shadow
Of Gitchie Manitou, the Mighty;
Where our braves can in the sunset,
In the shadow of their wigwams,
Smoke their pipes of peace together.

OUR COUNTRY'S SEASONS.

[*For four Girls or Boys.*]

Spring.

With March comes in the pleasant Spring,
When little birds begin to sing;
To build their nests, to hatch their brood,
With tender care provide them food.

Summer.

And Summer comes with verdant June:
The flowers, then, are in full bloom;
All nature smiles, the fields look gay;
The weather's fine to make the hay.

Autumn.

September comes: the golden corn
By many busy hands is shorn;
Autumn's ripe fruits, an ample store,
Are gathered in, for rich and poor.

Winter.

Winter's cold frost, and northern blast—
This is the season that comes last:
The snow has come, the sleigh-bells ring,
And merry boys rejoice and sing.

UNCLE NATHAN'S INDIAN.

Characters.—UNCLE NATHAN, *an Old Settler;* UNCLE CHRIS, *his Brother;* TOM, *aged* 12, BILL, *aged* 10, *their Nephews.*

SCENE.—*Room in* UNCLE NATHAN'S *house.*

Tom. Uncle Nathan, you promised us boys that if we wouldn't pester you when you were husking corn, you would take an evening and answer our questions about settling up the backwoods. Now, here it is almost Christmas and we haven't heard from you yet.

Uncle Nathan. Who is to blame, Tom, you or I, eh?

Tom. No matter now, expect we boys are. Well, were there Indians here when you came?

Uncle Nathan. Indians! Guess there were. Right across the river, not more than a mile from here, there was a camp of over two hundred.

Tom. What—real wild Indians?

Uncle Nathan. To be sure they were.

Tom. And did they ever scalp anybody? Weren't you afraid? Did they have bows and arrows and tomahawks and scalping-knives?

Uncle Nathan. Nobody was ever scalped to my knowledge. We used to be somewhat fearful at first, but we soon found out that they were either afraid, or had no disposition to hurt us. They had bows and arrows, and some guns, and tomahawks, and long knives which they used for dressing game.

Bill. O, Tom, wouldn't you like to see an Indian—a real bloody, wild Indian?

A rap at the door, which UNCLE NATHAN *opens, and* UNCLE CHRIS *enters, disguised as an Indian, his face colored a reddish brown.*

Uncle Chris (*stepping back a little into the darkness*). Whoo-o-o-o-o-p!

Tom and Bill (*starting for the stairs*) Oh, dear! he's an Indian.

Uncle Nathan. Come back, boys, he wont hurt you. Come in, Wild Cat.

Uncle Chris (*laughing*). Pappoosies big scare, oogh! Big Injun no kill pappoosie—no kill squaw—kill schmaukie man, oogh!

Bill (*whispering to his uncle*). Oh, I'm afraid he'll kill you, 'cause you *smoke*. Hide your pipe, uncle, for fear he does.

Uncle Nathan (*taking the pipe from his pockets and handing it to* Uncle Chris). Have a smoke, Wild Cat?

Uncle Chris. Oh! schmaukie man much good. Heap tobacco, big pipe. *Any wiskee?*

Uncle Nathan. No whiskey to-night.

Uncle Chris (*sorrowfully*). Oogh! Wild Cat much cold. Moccasin no good. *Blanket, oh, much hole.* Wiskee make warm, come—make no shiver. Leetle much wiskee, eh?

Uncle Nathan (*shaking his head*). No whiskey.

Uncle Chris. Schmaukie man no good. Poor Injun want wiskee—make warm come—Injun much money—much fight. No wiskee? Injun take pappoosies, eh? Schmaukie man give wiskee, get pappoosies back (*makes a spring, catches* Tom *and* Bill *and starts for the door.*)

Tom. Murder! Murder! MURDER!

Bill. Oh! *we'll be scalped!*

Uncle Nathan. Hold on, Chris, enough, enough; let them go.

Uncle Chris. How do you like a real, bloody, wild Injun, Bill?

Bill (*a little sulky*). You aint an Indian. Indians wouldn't scare little boys like you did me.

Uncle Chris. Come now, Bill, let us be friends again. Here is a book about the Indians, that I bought for you the other day. Wont that pay for your big scare? And I'll sit down and behave myself the rest of the evening. Come, let us make up.

Tom. All right. Hurrah for Wild Cat, the celebrated Flat-head Chief! Had any roasted dog to-day, Wild Cat?

Uncle Nathan. Now, boys, don't be too hard on Uncle Chris, for I engaged him to favor us with an Indian performance to-night, and he has done nobly. Old Wild Cat himself couldn't have surpassed him in playing his part. Come, Billy, let us have your opinion of a real, bloody, wild Indian.

Bill. I've got over my scare now, and I want to know if that was the way the Indians used to talk, and did they yell like that ?

Uncle Nathan. When we came here forty years ago, the Indians had traded with the white people enough to understand the English language, and speak it about as well as your uncle did to-night. Some, of course, got hold of it more readily, and others again were very hard to be understood. Uncle Chris is a fair, average Indian.

Tom. What did they live on ? Did they farm any ?

Uncle Nathan. Many years ago they had some cornfields on the river bottom. Wherever they had a village, there was usually a small field close by, where the squaws raised corn, beans, and sometimes pumpkins.

Tom. The squaws! Hey, Wild Cat, does your squaw raise *your* corn for you ? Wouldn't Aunt Em. "raise cane" if her "big Injun" wanted her to hoe corn ?

Bill. Hush, Tom, Uncle Nathan is full of talk; let us hear what he has to say.

Uncle Nathan. They depended on their guns and bows for most of their living. I have seen a young Indian shoot a bluebird with his bow and arrow, pull a few feathers off, and roast it on a rod over the smoke and fire, and then eat it.

Tom. Mighty nice, Uncle Wild Cat. How'll you take your bluebird ? feathers off, or roasted whole ?

Uncle Chris. Tom, I'm afraid you are not truly thankful to me for showing off the Indian to-night.

Tom. Oh yes! Much obliged to you, Mr. Wild Cat, for scaring me out of a year's growth. Wont you oblige me by taking off my scalp ? Would it be too much trouble to roast me to death, and dance around me while I'm burning ? Would you have some "wiskee" to get drunk on ? Now please do favor us with one of your delightful whoops before going to your wigwam to beat your squaw, and scare your poor orphanless pappoosies to death.

Uncle Chris. I give it up, Tom; and if I didn't see the fun in your eyes, I should feel sorry that I had come over here to-night to play the Indian, or the fool, whichever you please to call it.

Tom (laughing). There, now Uncle Chris, I'm even with you. You made me believe you were an Indian, and I made you believe I was mad about it, so after we've had one a-piece of Uncle Nathan's bell-flower apples we'll go home, and leave an appointment to hear the rest next week.

Uncle Nathan (passing the apples). In order to make you prompt next week, I will tell you that I bought the tree on which these apples grew of "Old Johny Appleseeds," who was a great character in the early day. *(Curtain.)*

THE MAY-BASKET ARMY.

Characters.—LUCY WHITE, JANE BLUE, MARY PINK, DOLLY BLACK, JOHN DIX, JOSEPH RAY, THOMAS DIKE.

[*Four little girls, dressed in White, Pink, Blue, and Black, seated at a table strewn with tissue paper. Each little girl has a May-basket.*]

Enter their TEACHER. *The children rise and approach her with their baskets.*

Teacher. My dear girls, I am delighted to see you all together here. 'Tis pleasanter and more social making your baskets in company. Are they complete?

Pink. We had just finished them as you came in; and we have been so happy in making them. Are they not pretty?

Teacher. They are very beautiful. Please hold them all up so that I can see them. The pattern is the same, but the colors different.

Pink. Yes; I made mine pink, or perhaps it is red, because that is my favorite color. You know the sun is always red when it is warm; and blushes are red, and blushes come straight from the heart, and love is in the heart, so I think love is red, and love is the best thing in the world: the Bible says so.

Teacher. Where did you find that in the Bible?

Pink. Well, the Bible says, "God is love."

Teacher. Yes, my dear child, "God is love," and love is the best thing in the world; and 'tis love makes heaven.

Pink. I know that. Grandma and our baby are all love; and Auntie says they are our heaven.

Blue. I made mine blue, teacher, because the sky is blue, and blue is the most beautiful color there is.

Teacher. And why do you think blue the most beautiful color?

Blue. I cannot tell. But I never tire looking at the beautiful sky. I see the sun there, and all the stars, and the moon. And when those light, fleecy clouds go sailing by, I think bright angels are in them.

White. I made mine white because you told me innocence and purity were clothed in white. Then white, you know, always looks so bright and clean. Little lambs are white, and little babies are dressed in white, and I love them. Everything white looks so pure.

Teacher. You three have made a good selection of colors; but how is it with Blackey? She looks like a dark shadow here.

Black. O, teacher, I made my basket black on purpose. You see 'tis made of coarse paper, and just put together anyway. I am going to give it to Phœbe Doler. Phœbe is a coarse girl, and rough in her manners, and she has an ugly face, and they are poor people.

Teacher. Is this a good reason for giving her a coarse, ugly May-basket?

Black. I should think so; it looks just like her.

Teacher (*takes the basket and examines it*). What an ugly basket this is! Who could have made a thing so entirely devoid of all beauty?

Black. I made it. But then I made it for Phœbe Doler.

Teacher. Blackey, I do not understand you. You are not a bad girl; you have not a bad heart; and I do not understand how you could have made so bad a basket.

Black. O, I made it for Phœbe Doler.

Teacher. It makes no difference who you made it for, since it is a gift; and a gift is a child of the heart. I did not think your heart could send forth into the world such an ugly child.

Black. But it is for Phœbe Doler.

Teacher. Phœbe Doler didn't make this basket. It is your child; you made it; and I am pained that you should allow such a bad feeling in your heart to take form and come forth into the world. Do you think it as pretty as Pinkey's.

Black. Not half; but then, it is for Phœbe Doler.

Teacher. Do you think Phœbe Doler is pretty?

Black. No, she has an ugly face; 'tis covered with freckles.

Teacher. And, you say, your basket looks just like her. I saw this morning, an ugly weed growing in my garden. I pulled it up and burned it.

Black. And would you burn this basket?

Teacher. I would, by all means; and then I would watch my heart very closely, and never again let it give form to anything that was not beautiful. (*Exit* BLACK.)

Enter three Boys, with bonnets and shawls on.

John. Teacher, we heard of this May army, and so we procured ourselves uniforms, and have come to ask your permission to enlist as soldiers.

Teacher. The addition of so many "braves" to our army would increase our strength. Your uniform may answer; but there are other things necessary to fit you for a place in our ranks.

Joseph. We were aware of this, and have come prepared. Question us, if you please.

Teacher. Do you know we are a May-basket army?

All. We do.

Teacher. Are you prepared with baskets for an evening's march?

All. We are.

Teacher. The spirit of our army is, to bless. Is there a blessing in your baskets?

All. We believe so.

Teacher. I see no objections to your entering our ranks, but I will leave the decision to Pinkey.

Pink. We will not accept them until we see their baskets.

(*Exeunt Boys.*)

Blue. That was a wise decision, Pinkey: those boys looked full of mischief, with their bonnets on.

White. But they are good boys. Sammy Ray would never do a wicked thing.

Re-enter Boys.

John (*with a basketful of potatoes*). Will not this basket of roots be a blessing to poor Mrs. Castaway?

Teacher. Indeed it will. You have complied with the spirit of our army; and though we see no delicate beauty in your rough basket, we know a living beauty is in the heart of it.

Joseph. My basket has a turkey in it. It is to go with the potatoes to Mrs. Castaway, for a bit of a relish.

Teacher. A double blessing for the poor woman. You "braves" will give strength to our army. Your baskets are substantial. Now for Soldier Third.

Thomas. My basket is a small one, and yet it contains what may be converted into tea, coffee, candles or snuff, as poor Mrs. Castaway may choose. (*he pours upon the table a hundred pennies.*)

Teacher. The poor woman will not think she is a castaway when she finds this trio of gifts at her door. Now, Pinkey, what is your decision? Shall we receive these bonneted volunteers into our army or not?

Pink. O, yes, we will receive them, but not their bonnets. I fear mischief in those comical bonnets.

Blue. Don't be over-particular, Pinkey. You mistake a little innocent fun for mischief. Since their baskets are all right, don't mind their bonnets.

Thomas. There is no mischief in our bonnets. Are they not after the same pattern as your own? Are they not in uniform?

Pink. Uniform is not always harmony. Bonnets do not harmonize with your heavy baskets, neither do they harmonize with your boy-nature. Teacher, order them to take off their bonnets.

Teacher. Pinkey, since you and Bluey differ in this matter of bonnets, we will let Whitey decide.

White. I am so much pleased with this addition of substantiality to our army, that I would like to indulge these generous volunteers in all their sportive whims.

Thomas. White fairy! your wish is our law. You have only to speak, and we obey.

White. Thank you, good soldier. We girls do not like apes; but we like *boys*. (*the boys lay their bonnets at her feet.*)

Pink. Bravo, boys! that is well done. Now all is right. I'll pick up your bonnets, and keep them for some poor girls that have none.

Enter BLACK, *smiling, dressed in scarlet with a scarlet basket; all gently applaud.*

Teacher. The dark cloud has given place to a warm, glowing sunbeam. Now you have a beautiful basket; the heart is all right; this one will please poor Phœbe Doler.

Black. I know it will. I don't think she ever had a pretty thing given to her in all her life. Perhaps it will do her good. I will try it any way.

Teacher. This trying it will do you good.

Black. And don't you think it will do Phœbe Doler good too?

Teacher. Certainly I do. Every kind word spoken, and every beautiful or useful gift carries a blessing in its heart.

Pink. I am delighted with our May-basket army. Susie Blackey has changed to Scarlet. All is right; and I know how to manage the affair. We must hang our baskets on the door knob, then ring the bell and run. We must go in the evening, so that the darkness will conceal us.

Blue. That's the way to do it, Pinkey—angels never show themselves when they leave a gift.

Thomas. When shall we commence our march?

Pink. As soon as you have gathered up your pennies. We are all ready. I shan't tell who I am going to hang my basket for—'tis somebody that will be pleased with it..

White. I am going to hang mine for grandpa; he is so good, and I know it will please him.

Pink. Grandpa! He is an *old* man. Why don't you hang it for some boy that you like?

White. Grandpa isn't *old*. He has lived a great many years, but that don't make him old; and I like him better than I do any of the boys.

Thomas. That is a hard cut, Fairy. I wish I were grandpa.

White. Can't I hang mine for grandpa?

Teacher. To be sure you can, if you think it would give him pleasure.

White. I know it would. Bluey, who are you going to hang yours for?

Blue. 'Tis for some one that I like very much, but I had rather not tell her. Pinkey would only laugh at me. But he is a good boy, and he is sick.

Thomas. I wish I were a good boy and sick. My pennies are all picked up. Are we ready to commence our march?

Teacher. You are all ready, and I wish you a pleasant evening. (*Exeunt.*)

IMAGINARY POSSESSIONS.

Characters.—BILL BUMPKIN. SOL BLUNT. CLEM CLODPOLL.

SCENE.—*A road. Enter* BILL *and* CLEM, *meeting.*

Bill. Hi, Clem, that you? You're late.

Clem. So be you; what kep' you?

Bill. I've been a-mowin' for Farmer Nabob; and I was bound to get done, if it took till bed-time. Where have you been?

Clem. Drivin' Uncle Jake's ox-team to the saw-mill. Ain't it a pretty night?

Bill. 'Tis that. Nary cloud to be seen.

Clem. Plenty of stars, though.

Bill. There's a mighty wide stretch of blue up there. I wonder how many acres there be in the sky. I wish it was all one big field of blue-grass, and I owned it.

Clem. Tell you what I wish. I wish all them stars was fat cattle, and they belonged to me.

Bill. Cattle! What in creation would you do with so many cattle? Where would you keep 'em?

Clem. Wall, I reckon I'd leave 'em in your big pasture.

Bill. Guess you'd better ask me about that; what rent would you pay?

Clem. I sha'n't pay at all, and I sha'n't ask leave.

Bill. Won't pay for pasterin' all them cattle?

Clem. Not a nickel.

Bill. Then, I'll shoot your blamed old cattle; every skin of 'em!

Clem. Shoot! I'd like to catch you at it; I'd kick you till you couldn't stand up!

Bill. Kick me! You, Clem Clodpoll, kick me? No, sir-ee; you're not the man to kick Bill Bumpkin. I'll shoot your cattle, old and young, horned and muley,—and if I ever see you within a hundred yards of my pasture, I'll——

Clem. I dare you to! Who's afraid of you? I'll tear down the fence; I'll burn your blue-grass; I'll haul stones all over your pasture-field!

Bill. You miserable, low-lived ox-driver. You're mean and sneakin' enough to steal or do any thing contemptible.

Clem. You're a liar, and a fightin' liar, and you daresn't take it up.

Bill. Take that. (*strikes* Clem; *they tussle and fight in the most boorish manner, and finally roll on the ground together.*)

Enter Blunt.

Blunt. What's all this? Get up, here, you young grizzly bears. Why are you fighting? (*he parts them. They stand, looking foolish, and rubbing their bruises*) Can't one of you speak? What was the cause of this moonlight encounter?

Clem. He said he'd shoot my cattle.

Bill. He said he'd burn my blue-grass.

Clem. He called me a thief.

Bill. He said he'd turn his cattle into my meadow without asking me.

Blunt. Cattle? Blue-grass? Meadow? What are you talking about? I didn't know that you owned any cattle.

Clem (*looking confused*). No, I don't; but, if I did——

Blunt. If you did? Ha, ha,—You don't mean to say you have been pommelling each other about an *if!* How is it, Bill; where is your meadow upon which Clem has been trespassing?

Bill (*scratching his head*). I'll tell you how it was, Sol; I said I wished the sky was a big pasture, and that it was mine; and Clem said he wished all the stars were cattle, and belonged to him.

Blunt. Yes.

Bill. Then we went on from one thing to another, till we got to thinking that sky *was* mine, and the stars *his'n.* Then we got to quarrelin' about our property, and I as good as called Clem a thief, and he as good called me a liar——

Clem. And so we fit.

Blunt. Well, that's the queerest cause of war that I ever heard about. You are more foolish than the men who disputed about the color of the chamelion. Shake hands, you blockheads, and go home. (*to audience*) Ladies and gentlemen, I don't wonder that you laugh at the absurd spectacle just exhibited before you. But I leave it to you, who are judges of human nature, to pardon the extravagance of our play, in view of the moral it conveys to those who are tempted to contend about Imaginary Possessions.

(*Curtain.*)

THE GRIDIRON.

[*The* CAPTAIN, PATRICK, *and the* FRENCHMAN.]

Patrick. Well, Captain, whereabouts in the wide world *are* we? Is it Roosia, Proosia, or Jarmant oceant?

Captain. Tut, you fool, it's France.

Pat. Tare an' ouns! do you tell me so? And how do you know it's France, Captain dear?

Capt. Because we were on the coast of the Bay of Biscay when the vessel was wrecked.

Pat. Troth, I was thinkin' so myself. And now, Captain, jewel, it is I that wishes we had a gridiron.

Capt. Why, Patrick, what puts the notion of a gridiron into your head?

Pat. Becase I'm starving with hunger, Captain dear.

Capt. Surely, you do not intend to eat a gridiron, do you?

Pat. Ate a gridiron! bad luck to it! No. But, if we had a gridiron we could dress a beefsteak.

Capt. Yes; but where's the beefsteak, Patrick?

Pat. Sure, couldn't we cut it off the pork?

Capt. I never thought of that. You are a clever fellow, Patrick. (*laughing.*)

Pat. There's many a thrue word said in joke, Captain. And now, if you'll go and get the bit of pork that we saved from the wrack, I'll go to the house there beyant, and ax some of them to lind me the loan of a gridiron.

Capt. But, Patrick, this is France, and they are all foreigners here.

Pat. Well, and how do you know but I am as good a furriner myself as any o' them?

Capt. What do you mean, Patrick?

Pat. Parley voo frongsay?

Capt. O, you understand French then, is it?

Pat. Troth, you may say that, Captain dear.

Capt. Well, Patrick, success to you. Be civil to the foreigners, and I will be back with the pork in a minute. (*he goes out.*)

Pat. Aye, sure enough, I'll be civil to them; for the French are always mighty p'lite intirely, and I'll show them I know what good manners is. Indade, and here comes munseer himself, quite convaynient. (*as the* FRENCHMAN *enters* PATRICK *takes off his hat, and, making a low bow, says*) God save you, sir, and all your children. I beg your pardon for the liberty I take, but it's only being in disthress in regard of ateing, that I make bowld to trouble ye; and, if you could lind me the loan of a gridiron, I'd be intirely obleeged to ye.

Frenchman (*staring at him*). Comment!

Pat. Indade, it's thrue for you. I'm tathered to paces, and God knows I look quare enough; but it's by rason of the storm, that dhruv us ashore jist here, and we're all starvin'.

French. Je m'yt—— (*pronounced* je meet.)

Pat. O! not at all! by no means! we have plenty of meat ourselves, and we'll dhress it, if you'd be plased jist to lind us the loan of a gridiron, sir. (*making a low bow.*)

French. (*staring at him, but not understanding a word.*)

Pat. I beg pardon, sir; but may be I'm undher a mistake, but I thought I was in France, sir. Ain't you all furriners here? Parley voo frongsay?

French. Oui, monsieur.

Pat. Then, would you lind me the loan of a gridiron, if you plase? (*the* FRENCHMAN *stares more than ever, as if anxious to understand*) I know it's a liberty I take, sir; but it's only in the regard of bein' cast away; and, if you plase, sir, parley voo frongsay?

French. Oui, monsieur; oui.

Pat. Then would you lind me the loan of a gridiron, sir, and you'll obleege me.

French. Monsieur, pardon, monsieur——

Pat. (*angrily*). By my sowl, if it was you was in disthress, and if it was to owld Ireland you came, it's not only the gridiron they'd give you, if you axed it, but something to put on it too, and a dhrop of drink into the bargain. Can't you understand your own language? (*very slowly*) Parley—voo—frongsay—munseer?

French. Oui, monsieur; oui, monsieur, mais——

Pat. Then lind me the loan of a gridiron, I say, and bad scram to you.

French. (*bowing and scraping*). Monsieur, je ne l'entend——

Pat. Phoo! the divil sweep yourself and your *long tongs!* I don't want a tongs, at all at all. Can't you listen to rason?

French. Oui, oui, monsieur; certainement, mais——

Pat. Then lind me the loan of a gridiron, and howld your prate. (*the* FRENCHMAN *shakes his head, as if to say he did not understand; but* PATRICK, *thinking he meant it as a refusal, says, in a passion*) Bad cess to the likes o' you! Troth, if you were in my counthry, it's not that-a-way they'd use you. The curse o' the crows on you, you owld sinner! The divil another word I'll say to you. (*the* FRENCHMAN *puts his hand on his heart, and tries to express compassion in his countenance*) Well, I'll give you one chance more, you owld thafe! Are you a Christhian, at all at all? Are you a furriner that all the world calls so p'lite? Bad luck to you! do you understand your mother-tongue? Parley voo frongsay? (*very loud*) Parley voo frongsay?

French. Oui, monsieur; oui, oui.

Pat. Then, thunder and turf! will you lind me the loan of a gridiron? (*the* FRENCHMAN *shakes his head, as if he did not understand; and* PAT *says vehemently*) The curse of the hungry be on you, you owld nagurly villain! the back of my hand and the sowl of my fut to you! May you want a gridiron yourself, yet! and, wherever I go, it's high and low, rich and poor, shall hear of it, and be hanged to you.

THE DISCONTENTED GIRLS.

Characters.—JENNIE, FLORA, *two little girls.*

SCENE.—FLORA *and* JENNIE *standing, with dirty faces, tangled hair, shoe-strings untied; one with a bonnet on, and the other swinging hers in her hand; and each carrying a load of school books.*

Jennie. So, you are ready for school, are you? I see you have got your bonnet and books.

Flora. Yes, I s'pose I've got to go, whether I want to or not. The plagued old school! I don't care a cent for it. All I do is get scolded! When I am at home mother scolds all the time; and when I am at school the teacher scolds. It's scold, scold, scold, all the whole time, from daylight till darkness. I am glad when it's time to go to bed, so I won't hear any more scolding; and I tell you, I lie as late in the morning as possible. Mother keeps calling me to get up, but I know how to fix *her.* I just stuff the bed-clothes in my ears, just as tight as I can; and then she calls and calls, and I never hear a single word!

Jennie. That's just the way I do too! I look out how I get up before breakfast! I can do work enough afterwards, and get scolding enough too. I have to hold the baby all the time, and all he does is squall, and then mother scolds; but I don't care! I make him squall sometimes on purpose! I hate babies, and I wouldn't take care of them if I could help it! I am glad when school-time comes, so as to get away from them. It's not quite so bad there, but it's bad enough, for it's study, study, study! I can't look off the book a single minute but the teacher sees me; and then those terrible geography lessons, with all those long hard names. I can *never* learn them. I suppose I shall have to stay after school every night, but I don't know as I care.

Flora. I just know what I wish. I wish I was a grown-up young lady. I would go to all the dances and parties I wanted to. I guess I'd do as I pleased then! I'd have just as many dresses as I wanted. I'd not wear an old flannel dress like this; and I'd have such beautiful feathers and ribbons! Oh, I'd cut a dash, I tell you! (*Exit both together.*)

DE WITT'S ACTING PLAYS.

(CONTINUED.)

103. Faust and Marguerite. A Drama, in three Acts. By T. W. Robertson. Nine Male, Seven Female Characters. Price.....................15 cts.

104. No Name.—A Drama, in four Acts. By Wilkie Collins. Seven Male, five Female Characters. Price................15 cts.

105. Which of the Two.—A Comedietta, in one Act. By John M. Morton. Two Male, ten Female Characters. Price....15 cts.

106. Up for the Cattle Show.—A Farce, in one Act. By Harry Lemon. Six Male, two Female Characters. Price.15 cts.

107. Cupboard Love.—A Farce, in one Act. By Frederick Hay. Two Male, one Female Character. Price..........15 cts.

108. Mr. Scroggins.—A Farce, in one Act. By William Hancock. Three Male, three Female Characters. Price........15 cts.

109. Locked In.—A Comedietta, in one Act. By J. P. Wooler. Two Male, three Female Characters. Price..................15 cts.

110. Poppleton's Predicaments.—A Farce, in one Act. By Charles M. Rae. Three Male, six Female Characters. Price......................15 cts.

111. The Liar.—A Comedy, in two Acts. By Samuel Foote. Altered and adapted by Charles Matthews. Seven Male, two Female Characters. Price....15 cts.

112. Not a Bit Jealous.—A Farce, in one Act. By T. W. Robertson. Three Male, three Female Characters. Price.15 cts.

113. Cyril's Success.—A Comedy, in five Acts. By H. J. Byron. Nine Male, five Female Characters. Price........15 cts.

114. Anything for a Change.—A Petite Comedy, in one Act. By Shirley Brooks. Three Male, three Female Characters. Price.............15 cts.

115. New Men and Old Acres.—A Comedy, in three Acts. By Tom Taylor. Eight Male, five Female Characters. Price....................15 cts.

116. I'm Not Mesilf at all.—An Original Irish Stew. By C. A. Maltby. Three Male, two Female Characters. Price....15 cts.

117. Not Such a Fool as he Looks.—A Farcical Drama, in three Acts. By H. J. Byron. Five Male, four Female Characters. Price................15 cts.

118. Wanted, a Young Lady.—A Farce, in one Act. By W. E. Suter. Three Male Characters. Price..........15 cts.

119. A Life Chase.—A Drama, in five Acts. By John Oxenford. Fourteen Male, five Female Characters. Price................15 cts.

120. A Tempest in a Teapot.—A Petite Comedy, in one Act. By Thomas Picton. Two Male, one Female Character. Price......................15 cts.

121. A Comical Countess.—A Farce, in one Act. By William Brough. Three Male, one Female Character. Price..15 cts.

122. Isabella Orsini.—A Romantic Drama, in four Acts. By S. H. Mosenthal. Eleven Male, four Female Characters. Price......................15 cts.

123. The Two Poets.—A Farce, in one Act. By John Courtney. Four Male, four Female Characters. Price...15 cts.

124. The Volunteer Review.—A Farce, in one Act. By Thomas J. Williams, Esq. Six Male, six Female Characters. Price ....15 cts.

☞ *Copies of any of the above Books will be sent, free of postage, on receipt of the retail price.*

Send Cash Orders to R. M. DE WITT, No. 33 Rose St., N. Y.

DE WITT'S
ACTING PLAYS.

(CONTINUED.)

125. **Deerfoot.**—A Farce, in one Act. By F. C. Burnand, Esq. Five Male, one Female Character. Price....................15 cts.

126. **Twice Killed.**—A Farce, in one Act. By John Oxenford. Six Male, three Female Characters. Price..............15 cts.

127. **Peggy Green.**—A Farce, in one Act. By Charles Selby. Three Male, ten Female Characters. Price............15 cts.

128. **The Female Detective.**—An Original Drama, in three Acts. By C. H. Hazlewood. Eleven Male, four Female Characters. Price............15 cts.

129. **In for a Holiday.**—A Farce, in one Act. By F. C. Burnand, Esq. Two Male, three Female Characters. Price....15 cts.

130. **My Wife's Diary.**—A Farce, in one Act. By T. W. Robertson. Three Male, one Female Character. Price....15 cts.

131. **Go to Putney.**—An Original Farce, in one Act. By Harry Lemon. Three Male, four Female Characters. Price....15 cts.

132. **A Race for a Dinner.**—A Farce, in one Act. By J. T. G. Rodwell. Ten Male Characters. Price....................15 cts.

133. **Timothy to the Rescue.**—An Original Farce, in one Act. By Henry J. Byron, Esq. Four Male, two Female Characters. Price..................15 cts.

134. **Tompkins the Troubadour.**—A Farce, in one Act. By Messrs. Lockroy and Marc Michel. Three Male, two Female Characters. Price.........15 cts.

135. **Everybody's Friend.**—An Original Comedy, in three Acts. By J. Stirling Coyne, Esq. Six Male, five Female Characters.

136. **The Woman in Red.**—A Drama, in three Acts and a Prologue. By J. Stirling Coyne, Esq. Six Male, eight Female Characters. Price.........15 cts.

137. **L'Article 47; or, Breaking the Ban.**—A Drama. In three Acts. By Adolphe Belot. Eleven Male, five Female Characters. Price..15 cts.

138. **Poll and Partner Joe; or, The Pride of Putney, and the Pressing Pirate.**—A new and original Nautical Burlesque. By F. C. Burnand. Seven Male, six Female Characters. Price...........15 cts.

139. **Joy is Dangerous.**—A Comedy, in two Acts. By James Mortimer. Three Male, three Female Characters. Price..15 cts.

140. **Never Reckon your Chickens.**—A Farce, in one Act. By Wybert Reeve. Three Male, four Female Characters. Price........................15 cts.

141. **The Bells; or, The Polish Jew.**—A Romantic Moral Drama, in three Acts. By Henry L. Williams, Jr. Nine Male, three Female Characters. Price...................15 cts.

142. **Dollars and Cents.**—An Original American Comedy, in three Acts. By L. J. Hollenius, Esq. Ten Male, four Female Characters. Price.........15 cts.

143. **Lodgers and Dodgers.**—A Farce, in one Act. By Frederick Hay. Four Male, two Female Characters. Price..15 cts.

144. **The Lancashire Lass; or, Tempted, Tried, and True.**—A Domestic Melodrama, in four Acts and a Prologue. By Henry J. Byron. Twelve Male, three Female Characters. Price..............15 cts.

145. **First Love.**—A Comedy, in one Act. By L. J. Hollenius, Esq. Four Male, one Female Character. Price.........15 cts.

146. **There's no Smoke Without Fire.**—A Comedietta, in one Act. By Thomas Picton. One Male, two Female Characters. Price.........15 cts.

☞ *Copies of any of the above Books will be sent, free of postage, on receipt of the retail price.*

Send Cash Orders to R. M. DE WITT, No. 33 Rose St., N. Y.

DE WITT'S
ACTING PLAYS.

(CONTINUED.)

147. The Overland Route.—A Comedy, in three Acts. By Tom Taylor. Eleven Male, five Female Characters. Price..15 cts.

148. Cut off With a Shilling.—A Comedietta, in one Act. By S. Theyre Smith. Two Male, one Female Character. Price......15 cts.

149. Clouds.—An Original American Comedy, in four Acts. By Fred Marsden. Eight Male, six Female Characters. Price..15 cts.

150. A Tell-Tale Heart.—A Comedietta, in one Act. By Thomas Picton. One Male, two Female Characters. Price..15 cts.

151. A Hard Case.—A Farce, in one Act. By Thomas Picton Two Male Characters. Price 15 cts.

152. Cupid's Eye-Glass.—A Comedy, in one Act. By Thomas Picton. One Male, one Female Character. Price......15 cts.

153. 'Tis Better to Live Than to Die.—A Petite Comedy, in one Act. By Thomas Picton. Two Male, one Female Character. Price......15 cts.

154. Maria and Magdalena.—A Play, in four Acts. By L. J. Hollenius, Esq. Ten Male, six Female Characters. Price......15 cts.

155. Our Heroes.—A Military Play, in five Acts. By John B. Renauld. Twenty-five Male, five Female Characters. Price..15 cts.

156. Peace at Any Price.—A Farce, in one Act. By T. W. Robertson. One Male, one Female Character. Price.....15 cts.

157. Quite at Home.—A Comedietta, in one Act. By Arthur Sketchley. Six Male, two Female Characters. Price....15 cts.

158. School.—A Comedy, in four Acts. By T. W. Robertson. Six Male, three Female Characters. Price......15 cts.

159. In the Wrong House; or, No. Six Duke Street.—A Farce. By Martin Becher. Four Male, two Female Characters. Price......15 cts.

160. Blow for Blow.—A Drama, in a Prologue and three Acts. By Henry J. Byron. Five Male, four Female Characters. Price......15 cts.

161. Woman's Vows and Masons' Oaths.—A Play, in four Acts. By A. J. H Duganne. Ten Male, four Female Characters. Price......15 cts.

162. Uncle's Will.—A Comedietta, in one Act. By S. Theyre Smith. Two Male, one Female Character. Price......15 cts.

163. Marcoretti; or, The Brigand's Sacrifice.—A Romantic Drama, in three Acts. By John M. Kingdom. Six Male, two Female Characters. Price......15 cts.

164. Little Ruby; or, Home Jewels.—A Romantic Drama, in three Acts. By J. J. Wallace. Six Male, six Female Characters. Price......15 cts.

165. The Living Statue; or, Chiselling.—A Farce, in one Act. By Joseph J. Dilley and James Allen. Three Male, two Female Characters. Price..15 cts

166. Bardell v. Pickwick (The Trial Scene from Pickwick.) A Farcical Sketch, in one Act. By Charles Dickens. Five Male, two Female Characters. Price......15 cts.

167. Apple Blossoms.—A Comedy, in three Acts. By James Albery. Seven Male, three Female Characters. Price....15 cts.

168. Tweedie's Rights.—A Comedy-Drama, in two Acts. By James Albery. Four Male, two Female Characters. Price..15 cts.

☞ *Copies of any of the above Books will be sent, free of postage, on receipt of the retail price.*

Send Cash Orders to R. M. DE WITT, No. 33 Rose St., N. Y.

DE WITT'S
ACTING PLAYS.
(CONTINUED.)

169. My Uncle's Suit.—A Farce, in one Act. By Martin Becher. Four Male, one Female Character. Price..........15 cts.

170. Only Somebody; or, Dreadfully Alarming.—A Farce, in one Act. By Conway Edwardes and Edward Cullerne. Four Male, two Female Characters. Price................15 cts.

171. Nothing Like Paste.—A Farce, in one Act. By Charles Marsham Rae. Three Male, one Female Character Price..15 cts.

172. Ours.—A Comedy, in three Acts. By T. W. Robertson. Six Male, three Female Characters. Price................15 cts.

173. Off the Stage.—An entirely original Comedietta, in one Act. By Sydney Rosenfeld. Three Male, three Female Charters. Price................15 cts.

174. Home.—A Comedy, in three Acts. By T. W. Robertson. Four Male, three Female Characters. Price....................15 cts.

175. Cast Upon the World. An entirely original Drama, in five Acts. By Charles E. Newton. Ten Male, five Female Characters. Price................15 cts.

176. On Bread and Water. —A Musical Farce, in one Act. By Sydney Rosenfeld. One Male, two Female Characters. Price....................15 cts.

177. I Shall Invite the Major.—A Parlor Comedy, in one Act. By G. von Moser. Four Male, one Female Character. Price................15 cts.

178. Out at Sea. An entirely original Romantic Drama, in a Prologue and four Acts. By Chas. E. Newton. Sixteen Male, five Female Characters. Price.15 cts.

179. A Breach of Promise. —An extravagant Comic Drama, in two Acts. By T. W. Robertson. Five Male, two Female Characters. Price........15 cts.

180. Henry the Fifth.—An Historical Play, in five Acts. By William Shakespeare. Thirty-eight Male, five Female Characters. Price................15 cts.

181 & 182. Queen Mary.—A Drama. By Alfred Tennyson. The only unmutilated edition. Arranged for the stage in four Acts. [The portions of the play to be omitted in representation are very carefully marked.] Edited by John M. Kingdom. Thirty-seven Male, nine Female Characters. This is a double number. Price................30 cts.

183. Richelieu; or, The Conspiracy.—A Play, in five Acts. By Sir Edward Lytton Bulwer. An entirely new acting edition. Twelve Male, two Female Characters. Price...15 cts.

184. Money.—A Comedy, in five Acts. By Sir Edward Bulwer. Sixteen Male, three Female Characters. Price.15 cts.

185. Not so Bad as We Seem; or, Many Sides to a Character.—A Play, in five Acts. By Sir Edward Lytton Bulwer. An entirely new acting edition. Thirteen Male, three Female Characters. Price.15 cts.

186. The Duchess de la Valliere.—A Play, in five Acts. By Sir Edward Lytton Bulwer. Six Male, four Female Characters. Price....................15 cts.

187. His Own Enemy.—A Farce, in one Act. By the author of "The Happy Pair" Five Male, one Female Character. Price....................15 cts.

188. Mr. X.—A Farce, in one Act. By Sydney Rosenfeld. Three Male, three Female Characters. Price....................15 cts.

189. Leap Year.—A Musical Duality. By Alfred B. Sedgwick. The music adapted from Offenbach's "Genevieve de Brabant." One Male, one Female Character. Price....................15 cts.

☞ *Copies of any of the above Books will be sent, free of postage, on receipt of the retail price.*

Send Cash Orders to R. M. DE WITT, No. 33 Rose St., N. Y.

DE WITT'S
ACTING PLAYS.
(CONTINUED.)

190. Hunting the Slippers; or, Painless Dentistry.—A Farce, in one Scene. By Martin Becher. Four Male, one Female Character. Price.... 15 cts.

191. High C.—A Comedietta, in one Act. By Sydney Rosenfeld. Three Male, two Female Characters. Price .... 15 cts.

192. A Game of Cards.—A Comedietta, in one Act. By L. J. Hollenius. Three Male, one Female Character. Price .... 15 cts.

193. My Walking Photograph.—A Musical Duality, in one Act. By Alfred B. Sedgwick. One Male, one Female Character. Price .... 15 cts.

194. Rum; or, The First Glass.—A Drama, in three Acts. By William Comstock. Seven Male, four Female Characters. Price .... 15 cts.

195. Rosemi Shell.—A Travesty (on "Rose Michel"), in four Scenes. By Sydney Rosenfeld. Six Male, three Female Characters. Price .... 15 cts.

196. The Queerest Courtship.—A Comic Operetta, in one Act. By Alfred B. Sedgwick. One Male, one Female Character. Price .... 15 cts.

197. The Hunchback.—A Play, in five Acts. By James Sheridan Knowles. Thirteen Male, two Female Characters. Price .... 15 cts.

198. The Twin Sisters.—A Comic Operetta, in one Act. By Alfred B. Sedgwick. Two Male, two Female Characters. Price .... 15 cts.

199. The Captain of the Watch.—A Comedietta, in one Act. By J. R. Planche. Six Male, two Female Characters. Price .... 15 cts.

200. Estranged.—An Operetta, in one Act. By Alfred B. Sedgwick. Two Male, one Female Character. Price .... 15 cts.

201. The School for Scandal.—A Comedy, in five Acts. By Richard Brinsley Sheridan. Thirteen Male, four Female Characters. Price .... 15 cts.

202. Eileen Oge.—An Irish Drama, in four Acts. By Edmund Falconer. Eleven Male, three Female Characters. Price........ .... 15 cts.

203. She Stoops to Conquer. A Comedy, in five Acts. By Oliver Goldsmith. Fifteen Male, four Female Characters. Price. 15 cts.

204. A Drawing Room Car. A Petite Comedy, in one Act. Two Male, one Female Character. Price.................... 15 cts.

205. Circumstances Alter Cases.—A Comic Operetta, in one Act. By Alfred B. Sedgwick. One Male, one Female Character. Price.................... 15 cts.

206. The Hair Apparent.—A Farce, in one Act. By Sydney Rosenfeld. Five Male, one Female Character. Price.... 15 cts.

207. Sold Again, and got the Money.—A Comic Operetta, in one Act. By Alfred B. Sedgwick. Three Male, one Female Character. Price..... 15 cts.

208. Married Bachelors.—A Comedietta, in one Act. By Sydney Rosenfeld. Three Male, two Female Characters. Price..................... 15 cts.

209. Othello.—A Tragedy, in five Acts. By William Shakspeare. Sixteen Male, two Female Characters. Price......... 15 cts.

210. Mabel's Manœuvre.—A Parlor Interlude, in one Scene. By Sydney Rosenfeld. One Male, three Female Characters. Price..................... 15 cts.

☞ *Copies of any of the above Books will be sent, free of postage, on receipt of the retail price.*

Send Cash Orders to R. M. DE WITT, No. 33 Rose St., N. Y.

GET THE BEST! GET THE BEST!

The farmer thinks no pains ill-bestowed in preparing the soil and selecting his seed, if he wishes for a bountiful harvest. How much more necessary is it to give earnest attention to the minds of the Little Folks! The love of reading is now so universal that there is a demand on the part of parents and guardians for the Best Reading Books, and we have spared neither time nor expense in producing

WEBSTER'S
LITTLE FOLKS' SPEAKER.

COMPRISING

Many Standard Pieces, as well as a great many entirely original, both Sentimental and Humorous.

This book is one of the worthiest of its kind. It contains **Two Hundred and Eleven Distinct Pieces**, in Prose and Poetry, carefully selected from the best Authors, expressly for Reading and Recitation in Primary as well as the next grade of Public and Private Schools.

Not only is this work of very superior literary merit, but the printing and binding are models of neatness and strength.

A careful examination of Webster's Little Folks' Speaker will convince that every article has been carefully culled, and is marked by true morality as well as by excellence of diction. It can be placed in a child's hand with the certainty that the contents will improve the morals, as well as refine and cultivate the taste.

This book contains 200 pages, bound in board, with a brilliant, illuminated cover. Price... ....50 Cents.
A handsome and durable edition, bound in cloth, elegantly lettered in gilt. Price..75 Cents.

☞ *Copies of the above Book sent to any address in the world, postage free, on receipt of price. Send Cash Orders to*

R. M. DE WITT, Publisher, 33 Rose st., N. Y.

(*Between Duane and Frankfort sts.*)

www.ingramcontent.com/pod-product-compliance
Lightning Source LLC
Chambersburg PA
CBHW020237170426
43202CB00008B/113